# MINDS IN MOTION

## THE CATALYST'S ROLE OF SPORTS PSYCHOLOGISTS



DR. CHAITANYA SRIDHAR,
KEERTHANA SWAMINATHAN

Clever Fox® PUBLISHING
Chennai • Bangalore

CLEVER FOX PUBLISHING
Chennai, India

Published by CLEVER FOX PUBLISHING 2025


Paperback ISBN: 978-93-6707-787-0
Hardback ISBN: 978-93-6707-733-7

This book is dedicated to the spirit of sports and the enduring odyssey of athletes, with special gratitude to those who guide and support them along the way.

# TESTIMONIALS

*"Sports psychologists are crucial for both performance and mental well-being. Dr. Chaitanya Sridhar helped me stay balanced and make rational decisions under pressure, proving that mental health is as important as physical fitness."*

**– Maana Patel, Olympic Backstroke Swimmer**

*"As an Olympian, I've learned that mental strength is as vital as physical preparation. Sports psychology helps manage pressure, enhance focus, and recover from setbacks. It has had a lasting impact on athletes' development, fostering both competitive spirit and personal resilience."*

**– Ashwini Nachappa, Olympian & Former Indian Athlete**

*"Bridging the gap between scientific knowledge and its real-world application is crucial in the development of athletes. By focusing on holistic, long-term athlete development and improving communication between parents, coaches, and athletes, we can ensure that psychological skills become an integral part of the sporting experience."*

**– Dr. Chris Harwood, Professor of Sport Psychology**

*"Nutrition is just as vital for mental resilience as it is for physical performance. By addressing deficiencies and inflammation, athletes can boost both cognitive function and emotional stability, unlocking their true potential for peak performance."*

**— Shiny Surendran, IOC-Certified Sports Nutritionist**

# CONTENTS

# FOREWORD

Through the 1990s, while finding my way through sports journalism, a word salad was offered up as the reason for widespread Indian sporting inadequacy at the international level: genetics, vegetarianism, lack of ambition ("only want jobs"), laziness and then the special one. Reserved for the very end: 'no killer instinct/ mental strength.' The people offering these facile responses knew that they would divert the attention of the most gullible from their governance failures.

Much we could dismiss. But in front of our eyes on TV screens or while reporting live on all manner of events, we could see our athletes and teams unravel at key moments, what they call 'clutch' these days. Sports journalism even had words for it – 'choking', 'meltdown' or 'bottling.' Golf termed it the 'yips.' Indian sport seemed to be ridden with 'snatching defeat from the jaws of victory' scenarios and narrow misses at the Olympic level. Why were some teams and individuals stronger at pushing through the stresses of competition while others couldn't? Why did India seem to have all the hard-luck stories? Even though 'killer instinct' was a loose and careless term, what was this thing called 'mental strength'? When almost every coach and guru said the game was x percent physical and 2x or 3x mental/ psychological/ temperamental, then why was no one looking into the heads and minds of our athletes?

Around that time every mention of 'sports psychology' or 'sports psychologists' emerged from overseas. Mostly around Olympic sports, featuring US athletes and then followed by the British and

Australians. The 1990s, remember, was still the pre-internet age. Even during that period, it is important to note that when Leander Paes turned pro in 1991, his wise and prescient father Dr Vece Paes' made sure he worked with noted psychologist Dr Jim Loehr.

At the time, Loehr was only known to Indians through a book, which I have re-discovered was called "Mental Toughness Training for Sport – Achieving Athletic Excellence." No question of getting hold of a copy back then, but Team Paes must be acknowledged as the first among leading Indian athletes to acknowledge the role of mental training in competitive sport.

The first sports psychologist we got to heard a little more about was Dr Sandy Gordon, who worked with the all-conquering Australian cricket team from the mid-1990s. When Gordon spent a few days with the Indian cricketers in the run-up to their first match at the 2003 ICC Cricket World Cup, it felt like a big leap.

We have gone from Paes and Dr Loehr, Sandy Gordon and the Indian cricket Team to now and this book. *Minds In Motion: the Catalyst's Role of Sports Psychologists* marks out the complete re-orientation of an aspect of Indian sport science over the last 25 years. During this period, the growth and development in this field has run alongside, and so may well be a contributor itself, to the rise of Indian sport across disciplines. The role of overseas psychologists in the early years post liberalization was very important in itself in bringing the field to greater public notice. But today, the comfort of an Indian sporting aide innately familiar with the peculiar cultural characteristics awash in our sport, has also given athletes of every layer a chance to pursue their individual paths to excellence.

It was to be several years and Olympics cycles from the Sandy Gordon intervention that the sporting ecosystem and the public was could fully fathom the importance of sports psychologists, mental conditioning coaches / trainers. More recently, in keeping with international trends, the emotional well-being of athletes has taken precedence over performance outcomes. What the arrival of the psychologist in our sporting ecosystem also did was to present a vital alterantive to the power dynamic that had been play for many decades in Indian sport. To us journalists from the outside, the presence of the psychologist indicated to everyone around that the requirement/s of the athlete / team was the most important issue in the room. Even though many athletes may still touch their coachs' feet, this is no mean thing. What's even better, this particular clock cannot be turned back.

*Dr. Chaitanya Sridhar and Keerthana Swaminathan* have done a fine job of gathering the body of work across Indian sports psychology and setting it in a very relevant context. This is a handsomely compiled, first-of-a-kind project whose findings and benefits will be mined decades from now. *Minds In Motion* is both a panoramic view of where Indian sports psychology finds itself today and a road map of the future explorations that lie ahead.

To many of us on the outside, our understanding sports psychology can be fairly surface and box-tick-y. Meditation, visualisation, therapy sessions. Tick, tick, tick. These are mere words. What *Mind In Motion* does is go into the granularity and nuances of the conversations both within and without both the athlete and psychologist and from athlete to psychologist and vice versa. The many layers that lie behind and underneath the words what we churn out in our business as sports journalists so flippantly as easy reasoning and supposedly informed assessment. Like team spirit, resilience, culture, sub-conscious, pressure, expectation, self-esteem, perfectionism, dedication, grit. But deconstructed and explained with the knowledge and sophistication of the expert. Much that is valuable is not permanent and so needs reinforcing, much that is deeply impactful must be kept at bay or cast aside.

The sports psychologists will tell you that one shape and size does not fit all – and this is even before applying even complex specificity of the Indian sporting landscape and the number of variables that each athlete brings to their team or their competition. Reading through *Mind in Motion* is getting like going through a crash-course of Indian Sports Psych101. Sometimes it is like eavesdropping on multiple conversations taking place amongst Indian sports psychologists - practitioners, teachers and students - and also with colleagues from other parts of neural network that comprises sports science in our country: orthopaedics, exercise science, recovery, nutrition, sociology. *Mind In Motion* is a rare insight into the mind of Indian athletes and the minds of their mind-teachers. It is educational, inspirational and humbling.

**– Sharda Ugra,**
*Sports Journalist*

# PREFACE

"Are you a counsellor?"

"Can you do a motivation session just before the competition?" "So, what advice can you give my athlete?"

"Would you tell me what the athlete is going through?" "Can you speak to my athlete before every competition?"

"Have you given any specific tools to work with so that I can monitor it?" "Oh, I can play the psychologist's role in your absence."

"I also counsel my kid."

These were put out not just to draw your attention, but these are also some of the narratives that exist in the ecosystem. These perspectives are quite limited, outdated, and irrelevant in this current day and age. There is too much emphasis on medals, rankings, and numbers that we miss out on the opportunity to look at and develop the athlete as a whole. This vacuum and biased focus on the outcome alone has led us into a state of fear of failure, disappointment, dejection, breakdowns, or even burnout and eventually not enjoying the very sport they had fallen in love with. For instance, during COVID-19, we as practitioners began to notice that there was a lot of anxiety and dissociation from themselves and their own lives.

When we ponder upon the evolution of the field of sport psychology in India, it has gradually shifted—quietly, yet steadily, and with immense heart. In its early days, the journey was marked by unfamiliarity and scepticism. Yet amid these uncertainties, a handful of practitioners began to forge pathways—building trust with athletes, adapting international frameworks to local realities, and most importantly, listening. They listened to the silences between words, to the stories behind performance dips, and to the unspoken struggles that often accompany sporting ambition.

*Minds in Motion: The Catalyst's Role of Sports Psychologist* was conceived as a space to document, celebrate, and critically reflect on those journeys.

It is a collection of voices—from practitioners who have worked in the field, often under-resourced but never under-committed. This is not a typical academic book. Nor is it a prescriptive handbook. Some chapters are reflective, others are practical. Some are built on frameworks, others on field notes and first-hand experiences. All are written with care, honesty, and a deep sense of responsibility to the profession and the people it serves.

What ties these narratives together is a belief in the catalytic role that sport psychologists can play—not only in enhancing performance, but in shaping cultures of well-being, resilience, inclusion, and ethical practice within Indian sport. The contributors come from diverse backgrounds, but they share common values: empathy, adaptability, curiosity, and the courage to question the status quo.

This book is for everyone who sees sport not just as a pursuit of medals, but as a medium for growth —for individuals, communities, and systems. It is to drive the narrative shift from focusing on just the outcome to the overall well-being, which is bound to bring sustainable dividends in all aspects of one's life, especially peak performance.

"I just feel very seen and heard talking to you"

"I started using the cue word that we created and I played very well."
"You transformed my life."

---

> *"The way I handle pressure and stress has positively changed."*
>
> **– This encapsulates the impact of what we do.**

---

A huge shout out to the athletes who trusted us with their stories, and to all those who continue to believe in the invisible but powerful work of the whole person—this is for you.

# INTRODUCTION

Sport psychology is making its way to the sporting ecosystem and claiming its space in sport science as a rightful integrated necessity. And yet, the work of sport psychologists often remains misunderstood, underrepresented, and fragmented. Even today, the sessions we do are largely reactive rather than proactive.

The book and its chapters aim to address this lacuna and integrate it into the system. In a gist, some of the aspects that is discussed - What does it actually look like to build trust with a teenage athlete from a tribal village? To introduce mindfulness in a cricket team riddled with performance anxiety? To navigate professional boundaries while travelling with elite athletes? To advocate for psychological safety within a system driven solely by results?

This book attempts to answer these questions—in context, and not in the abstract.

*Minds in Motion: The catalyst's role of Sports Psychologists* **is structured around three core sections:**

1. Performance, Pressure, and Support – Chapters in this section examine how psychological principles are applied to enhance performance, manage perfectionism, build mental toughness, and support resilience in the face of injury or failure.
2. Well-being and Practitioner Awareness – Here, contributors reflect on the mental well-being and health needs of athletes, the

emotional labour of sport psychologists, and the importance of supervision, boundaries, and gender-sensitive practice.

3. Ecosystem and Integration – This section zooms out to examine the broader system—exploring how pedagogy, sleep, nutrition, and injury management intersect with psychological support, and how we can build sustainable, interdisciplinary approaches to athlete care.

Each contribution is grounded in the Indian sporting context. Some authors write from national academies, others from grassroots initiatives. Some speak from lived experience as athletes themselves. Collectively, their voices offer a textured, honest, and hopeful view of what it means to do sport psychology in India today and in the future. We are grateful to all those who contributed to this volume and to the wider community, whose ongoing work continues to shape the field. This book builds on the foundations laid by many before us and looks ahead to the future of sport psychology in India.

## How to Use This Book

This book is meant to be a bridge—between theory and practice, between disciplines, and between generations of practitioners. Here are a few ways different readers might use it:

- **For students and early-career professionals:** Gain insights into the realities of applied sport psychology, explore ethical dilemmas, and learn how to adapt interventions to diverse athlete populations.
- **For athletes:** Deepen your understanding of the mental aspects of performance, build resilience through challenges, and explore ways to support your well-being on and off the field.
- **For coaches and support staff:** Understand the psychological undercurrents of performance and team dynamics, and explore how to co-create psychologically safe environments for athletes.

- **For federations and decision-makers:** Discover practical models for integrating psychology into talent development, high performance, and injury recovery systems.
- **For researchers:** Identify areas that require deeper study, and examine the lived intersections between psychological theory and real-world application.

This book does not offer one answer. It offers many questions—and the lived wisdom of those who have dared to ask them and opens the door to more reflections.

Welcome to the conversation for Indian Sport.

# AUTHOR INTRODUCTION

## DR. CHAITANYA SRIDHAR

Dr. Chaitanya Sridhar is a trailblazing Sports and Trans-species Psychologist with over 20 years of experience mentoring elite athletes—including Olympic medallists. She earned her PhD in Psychology in Australia and made history as the first woman sports psychologist in the IPL, working with Royal Challengers Bangalore in 2020. Her work has been recognised by the Ministry of Youth Affairs and Sports for its lasting impact on Indian high-performance sport.

A trusted advisor to INSPA and co-developer of India's first online sports science course with IIT-Madras, Dr. Sridhar continues to shape the field through education and innovation.

Outside of sport, she is the founder of All About Nature of Elephants (AANE), an initiative supporting elephant well-being. She also contributes to the rehabilitation of captive elephants. A TEDx speaker and author of Elephant Wings to Freedom, she brings together human and animal psychology to inspire empathy, resilience, and systemic change.

## KEERTHANA SWAMINATHAN

Keerthana Swaminathan is a leading sports psychologist whose work bridges science, cultural insight, and human connection.

She has worked across disciplines like cricket, badminton, and tennis—helping athletes enhance motivation, set meaningful goals, and perform under pressure.

Currently pursuing a PhD on psychological safety and athlete performance at the University of Staffordshire, she adopts a research-driven, athlete-first approach.

She is listed on the ISSP-R, and her previous work with an IPL franchise—alongside ongoing global collaborations—reflects her growing influence in the field.

As President of the Indian Sports Psychologists Association (INSPA), Keerthana champions ethical, culturally responsive practice. She also leads Project CARE, INSPA's initiative for athlete mental health and psychological first aid, and co-directs The Performance Doctor in Chennai, a multidisciplinary clinic fostering holistic athlete development across levels.

# CONTRIBUTORS

## MUGDHA A. BAVARE

Mugdha A. Bavare is a Sport and Counseling Psychologist with over two decades of experience working with elite Indian athletes across cricket, archery, shooting, wrestling, swimming, and more. A former national swimmer and recipient of the Shri Shiv Chhatrapati Award, she is the founder of *Mindsports*, focusing on mental training and performance enhancement.

She has worked with leading organisations such as the BCCI, National Cricket Academy, Mumbai Cricket Association, Olympic Gold Quest, and Army Yachting Node. She was the first sport psychologist appointed by the BCCI to travel with the Indian Women's Cricket Team for the 2022 ODI World Cup in New Zealand.

In 2024, Mugdha accompanied athletes to the Paris Olympics and served as the Welfare Officer for India's Paralympic contingent—an initiative by the International Paralympic Committee. She also supported the Indian Women's Cricket Team at the T20 World Cup in Dubai the same year. Mugdha is the author of the book *"Sports Psychology"* (2024) and co-founder of *Disha Counseling Center*, a mental health and vocational guidance center active for 25 years.

## VAIBHAV AGASHE

Vaibhav Agashe is a certified sport psychology consultant and Research Fellow with the American Board of Sport Psychology, with over 18 years of experience working with elite Indian athletes. He has served as a mental trainer for multiple Olympic medalists, including two shooters who won medals at the London 2012 Olympics and a medal-winning shooter at the 2024 Paris Olympics.

Vaibhav has provided psychological support to athletes across disciplines such as shooting, archery, tennis, badminton, chess, squash, golf, and athletics. He works closely with organisations including Olympic Gold Quest, the Sports Authority of India, and the National Rifle Association of India. His approach emphasizes on-field mental skills coaching, and he regularly travels with athletes to training camps and international competitions.

Through his boutique consulting practice, Vaibhav is committed to fostering peak performance and mental resilience in Indian sport.

## VARADAYINI CHITALE GHORE

Founder, MindFirst Performance, Co-Founder INSPA

ISSP-Registered Professional Sport Psychologist with a 13 year- wealth of experience in the Indian landscape of sport psychology. Having completed her Masters from Loughborough University in 2012, setting foot in a nascent world of sport psychology in India was the beginning of a very exploratory journey.

She enjoys working with young athletes, coaches and parents. She also likes to apply her knowledge to other high performing setups like the India Inc. Currently, her in depth reflections has helped her develop standardised sport psychology and mental health protocols and systems for HPCs through her work with Nudge Sports. Her research and interest lies in youth sports, culture as well as professional ethics.

In her spare time, she loves to run, write, read and sing!

## MAURELLE D'SA

With over nine years of experience in sport, performance, and behavior change settings, Maurelle is a Sport & Exercise Psychology consultant. She holds a Master of Science in Psychology of Sport & Exercise from Loughborough University, UK, and a Master of Arts in Psychology from the University of Mumbai, India. She has also completed an Advanced Practicum Training in Rational Emotive Behaviour Therapy (REBT) from the Albert Ellis Institute, New York, and its application with children from In Vivo, Mumbai.

Currently, Maurelle is a Doctoral Researcher and Graduate Teaching Assistant at Edge Hill University, UK, and serves as the Secretary of the Indian Sport Psychologists' Association (INSPA).

Her professional journey includes serving as the Consulting Sport Psychologist at several national organisations and private academies. She also works extensively with individual athletes at the national and international levels across various sports and age groups.

In academia, Maurelle has contributed as a visiting faculty member for Sport & Exercise Psychology courses at several institutions across the city and has been involved in several training programs for sport psychologists in India.

## PARTII PARASHER

Parth Parasher is currently practicing Sport Psychology in India. His main focus is developing positive youth development programs at residential schools all over the country. He has dual Masters degrees in Psychology and Sport Psychology from Glasgow and Loughborough University respectively. Previously he has worked with elite football academies in the UK and India applying context specific psychosocial skill development programs. In addition to Sport Psychology he has obtained Qualified Teacher Status from University of Buckingham. An avid trekker and climber Parth has finished his Mountaineering certifications from Himalayan Mountaineering Institute, Darjeeling.

## PRIYANKA PRABHAKAR

Priyanka Prabhakar is a psychologist based out of Bangalore. Priyanka has worked at Sports Authority of India as a Sports Psychologist. She has worked extensively with the Indian Hockey Men & Women's Teams during Rio Olympics 2016 & Tokyo Olympics 2020 respectively. She has been the first psychologist from India to travel abroad for a competition with the Indian Women's Hockey team. She has the experience of working with many elite athletes from multiple sport disciplines and has contributed to their wellness. Priyanka works on building high performance in sports and corporate. She uses a research and activity based approach. Priyanka works as a Guest faculty for Sports Psychology at Jain University and Sports Authority of India (SAI). She has curated a Sports Psychology course for NPTEL as an adjunct faculty of IIT-Madras. She works as a consultant with Nudge Sports Private Limited. Priyanka is a private practitioner and she is a trained Systemic and Family constellation Facilitator from Spanda Asia and Ochre Ireland.

## MUDIT KRISHNANI

Mudit is a sport and exercise psychology practitioner and educator based in India, with experience spanning grassroots to elite-level athletes. His professional interests lie in psychoeducation and the integration of technological advancements into sport psychology Practices. Committed to building sustainable high-performance cultures, Mudit takes a holistic, macro-level approach to athlete development and mental skills training across sport, e-sport and para sport. His work emphasizes long-term skill development and the psychological foundations of consistent elite performance.Passionate about bridging the gap between theory and applied practice, Mudit is dedicated to advancing sport psychology in India. His efforts aim to empower individuals to excel in the complex and demanding world of high performance.

## DR. SAHEN GUPTA

Dr. Sahen Gupta is a British Psychological Society (BPS) and Health and Care Professions Council (HCPC) accredited sport psychologist, currently serving as a Senior Lecturer in Applied Sport Psychology at the University of Portsmouth. He is the Founder and Head Consultant of Discovery Sport & Performance Lab and a Visiting Professor at the National Institute of Sport (NIS), India. Dr. Gupta has extensive experience working with elite athletes, having served as the Head Sport Psychologist for teams at ICC World Cups, European Qualifiers, and National Championships. His academic credentials include an MSc and Doctorate in Sport & Exercise Psychology from Glasgow Caledonian University, with his doctoral research focusing on resilience in high-performance environments. He is also a published author, contributing to titles such as *Cognitive Behaviour Therapy in Sport and Performance* and *Research Methods in Applied Sport Psychology*.

## VAISHALI CHAUDHARY

Vaishali Chaudhary is a counseling psychologist specializing in sports, with experience working with elite and non-elite athletes across individual, team, winter and water sports. She firmly believes that performance and mental health are deeply interconnected and that building a supportive ecosystem is essential for athletes to reach their full potential.

She has worked with the Inspire Institute of Sport and the Sports Authority of India, providing psychological support to athletes at various stages of their careers. Her approach goes beyond performance metrics—she sees athletes as individuals first, recognizing that their struggles often extend beyond the field.

Vaishali advocates for a collaborative approach to performance, where not just coaches but also support staff and parents play a crucial role in an athlete's development. She has conducted numerous workshops and has been a speaker at various sports events, sharing her insights on athlete well-being and mental resilience.

She finds immense joy in exploring the dynamics that emerge when athletes are given a safe space in group settings. To her, performance isn't just about reaching an optimal level but also about staying humble and embodying true sportsmanship. Passionate about creating spaces where athletes can embrace their identities beyond their sport, she continuously strives to help them reconnect with different parts of themselves—whether it's in a library, a game room, or painting in a garden.

## AYAN MRUGANK MERCHANT

Ayan is a Performance Consultant with seven years of experience supporting athletes in diverse sports. She earned a PhD in Cardiovascular Sciences from the University of Glasgow, focusing her research on sleep, dietary habits, and food choices. She also holds an MSc in the Psychology of Sport from the University of Stirling in Scotland and an MA specializing in Clinical Psychology from Maharaja Sayajirao University of Baroda in Vadodara. A graduate member of the British

Psychological Society, the British Association of Sports and Exercise Sciences, and the British Sleep Society, Ayan is also a certified practitioner of Cognitive Behavioural Therapy for Insomnia. Her work as a psychologist and management consultant reflects a practical approach. Ayan specialises in enhancing individual development and well-being, helping individuals reach peak performance. She has implemented numerous training programs and managed projects that emphasise leadership development and athlete performance. Additionally, she has authored and presented research on athlete development, coaching styles, and coach-athlete dynamics. Beyond her academic achievements, Ayan has a BA in Music with a concentration in Kathak Dance and has trained in field hockey, rugby, handball, and skiing.

## GAURI SHRINGAPURE

Gauri Shringarpure is a mental health practitioner specializing in positive psychology, self-care, and gender-sexuality training. With over 25 years of experience in consumer behavior research and ethnography, and more than one and a half decade of mental health work, she brings a unique perspective to her therapeutic practice. Gauri serves as faculty for the Mariwala Health Initiative's Queer Affirmative Counselling Practice (QACP) Certificate Course, where she trains mental health professionals in anti-oppressive, queer-affirmative therapeutic approaches. Her work focuses on integrating insights from consumer behavior and positive psychology into mental health practices, emphasizing self-care and well-being.

## AMALINA

Amalina has an educational background in psychology and social science, and has conducted research on a variety of social science topics. Through her work as a training associate at MHI, she is involved in the administration, impact assessment and research related to MHI's various training programs on marginalisation and gender-sexuality. Through her work and in her personal life, she is interested in advocating for queer-trans rights.

## PARINAAZ IRANI

Parinaaz Irani, a sport and performance psychologist is the founder of InnerPeak, a company focused on empowering leaders and performers towards balancing performance with wellbeing. With an educational background in both sport psychology and clinical psychology, she has worked with several athletes and coaches in in different sports, predominantly cricket, football, golf, ten track and field and badminton.

She is driven towards building a curriculums and ecosystems for academies to support their athlete's psychological health and overall growth alongside parents, coaches and sport science teams. Her areas of academic and research interests lie within leadership, perfectionism, eating and nutrition beliefs in athletes and building evidence-based programs for high-performance environments. Lastly, she aims to nurture the upcoming generations through education and guidance and is currently teaching sport psychology at academic institutions.Working as an entrepreneur, she values growth and failure as much as she does success. An amalgamation of care and grit, Parinaaz is focused towards providing inspiration and a pathway for individuals to become the best version of themselves.

SECTION I

# PERFORMANCE, PRESSURE, AND SUPPORT

---

*"We are what we repeatedly do. Excellence, then, is not an act but a habit."*

**– Aristotle**

---

# EXPERIENCES IN DIFFERENT LANDSCAPES IN INDIAN SPORTS - VAIBHAV AGASHE

The field of Sport Psychology has grown significantly in India over the past few years. It is encouraging to see students taking up Sport Psychology as a career option, and enrolling for studies in India and abroad. Sport Psychologists are being appointed across various sports. Indian sports require a large pool of Sport Psychologists to work with players at every level, from grassroots to national. Eventually, we will reach a point where sport-wise and even function-wise specialisations will be essential. This, in turn, will allow a team of professionals to work together, referring players for specialised training or specific phases of counselling.

We have come a long way in terms of overall awareness, but I started at a time when there were very few professionals in this field. Around 2003-04, The Sports Authority of India had a very good Sport Science Centre up in Jawaharlal Nehru Centre. The head of the Sport Psychology department at the time was the one who first evaluated my training programme and recommended it to various teams under SAI. This mentor was crucial in guiding my understanding of the visualization protocols that were followed at the time, and our interactions proved to be very beneficial for my professional journey.

Shooting was one of the first disciplines in which mental training came to be implemented in India extensively. Within shooting, Rifle shooters were the first to adopt it. Rifle shooting was a skill at which Indian athletes were very close to elite level, with some even reaching that standard. The elite shooters instinctively knew how important concentration and maintaining relaxation during the shot were, and they were determined to work on it.

In the early years, mind training was introduced during the national camps. Foreign coaches were quite receptive. When I first worked in the national camp in 2005, the rifle coach at the time interviewed me and enquired about which techniques I would implement. He made sure I was going to introduce the right ones. He asked me to focus on a select few mental skills and did not give a blind mandate. Then he introduced it to the team thoughtfully, making time for it and supporting the training programme.

In the subsequent years, other foreign coaches were also very supportive. They trusted the training provided clear briefings on how a shooter needs to think during training, and they also held one-on-one meetings with the shooters, in which I was included.

In the subsequent years, it was rare for athletes to take the initiative and hire a mind trainer, but elite players did, and they reaped the benefits. One athlete engaged in extensive personalised training not just with me, but with several other trainers. Another athlete continued to work hard even after winning the Olympic silver medal and took me along as a personal trainer for a long training and competition stint abroad. Later, before the London Olympics, Gagan

Narang made a serious effort to improve his mental skills over the entire year leading up to the London Games.

Some smart athletes treated this as a competitive edge and never spoke about it. One top shooter from the Shotgun side was very frank about it. While starting training with me, he told me after a couple of sessions that he would never tell anyone he was doing mind training. He said, "I know it is very effective and useful, I am benefiting tremendously because of it. Why should I let my competitors know?" For him, it was an edge over the competition. Now, the situation has changed completely—it is a level playing field.

Earlier, many didn't quite recognised the need for mental health support. It just wasn't something that was talked about. The awareness was low. It was a novelty. However, athletes as a whole have become more open-minded. The change is particularly significant after COVID-19. There is now much more awareness about mental health, and athletes are willing to openly talk about it. This is a welcome change, and the stigma around taking professional help is reduced to quite an extent.

The awareness about mind training among the officials of federations was low earlier. They had to be convinced to include a mind trainer with the team during training camps. The budget for sending a mind trainer with the team for competitions was always available with SAI, but the federations did not ask for it because of various reasons. But over the years, more and more teams have started budgeting for this and regularly send sports psychologists with the athletes. There is a change in expectations as well. Earlier, the approval of the budget was more for winning a medal; now, there is increasing awareness that it is a support service provided to athletes to deal with the overall stress of competitions.

The emergence of Independent sponsors like Olympic Gold Quest in 2009 was a big positive for Sport Psychology in India. Later, other organisations like Go Sports also came up. OGQ has been very supportive of all sport science professionals, including sport psychologists. They sponsored the training and travel, and it made sure that the elite athletes got support throughout the year, and it was not restricted only to national camps.

With these opportunities to travel with players for training and competitions, I travelled extensively—sometimes for months at a stretch. I spent a lot of time in the field observing players very closely. Taking extensive notes, writing down every single observation really helped.

Buying a professional camera along with a tripod to take pictures of shooters in action, recording videos, and documenting important moments during training, as well as competitions, required a lot of work, but it was worth it. These pictures/videos, along with handwritten notes, provided huge material to work with.

As the field of sports psychology in India evolved, so did the methods used to support athletes. While early challenges centred around awareness and acceptance, technological advancements have since played a crucial role in enhancing mental training. Tools like biofeedback, neurofeedback, and Athlete Monitoring Systems (AMS) have revolutionized how psychologists assess and support athletes, allowing for a more data-driven and personalised approach

Similarly, I have invested a huge amount of money in buying biofeedback and neurofeedback equipment over the years. Initially, I had bought Medicaid Systems equipment, and later, I switched to Thought Technology gear. They aren't cheap, and it was quite a stretch for me and my wife, who were both young professionals with a family to support, to afford them. But we never thought about any return on these investments from a commercial angle. We bought them because they were required to do the work professionally, and my athletes required these. Over time, I've continued to buy different types of sensors and use them.

My evidence-based and data-driven approach gained a theoretical framework when I pursued professional certification with the American Board of Sport Psychology under the guidance of Dr. Roland Carlsteft. His theory of personality, critical moments, and testing protocol provided a much-needed foundation for making sense of the data. Assisting Dr. Carlstedt on one of his large analytical projects also helped me immensely.

I can't say that I used these methods to their full potential. There are limitations, mainly due to how much time you get to spend with the athlete and the many tasks you need to handle. One has to be selective about which training method to follow.

Also, all athletes are not equally receptive to biofeedback. I have seen athletes like Gagan Narang who wanted to put every possible sensor on their body while shooting, and he could handle and incorporate the feedback coming from the equipment. On the other hand, I've also seen athletes who get overwhelmed by just one type of feedback and can't relate to it.

The prices of biofeedback and neurofeedback are still high today, and there aren't many good options available for home training with biofeedback. I have been waiting for a long time for a mobile-based system for home use, where Sport Psychologists can see the livestream of data during the session. I hope that such a system becomes available soon. As such, biofeedback/neurofeedback training modality is not being utilized to its full potential. This is one area where the availability of options for sport psychologists has not kept pace with what is possible technologically.

One of the biggest challenges that I faced when I travelled with the teams was to find enough time to train with athletes while they were still fresh. They were already quite busy in training sessions, physical training, and physiotherapy. You don't want to interfere with their rest and recovery by intruding into those

time slots. Although sport psychologists were included in the team, there was no specific time slot set aside for us in the weekly training calendar.

When you're working with multiple athletes, scheduling sessions in these limited time slots can be a challenge. Being very fair in booking time slots and honouring them is key to maintaining professionalism and neutrality. You have to deal with delicate issues, like athletes turning up late or sessions overlapping. You don't want to get caught up in the competitive instincts and rivalries between athletes. Sometimes it is good to use a scheduling /booking app that makes your time slots available publicly to get the job done.

Group sessions in large team settings also come with their own set of challenges. Many times, athletes turn up for a session tired and exhausted. They may struggle with attention and alertness. The moment you ask them to close their eyes, they doze off to sleep. It takes experience to anticipate these challenges and overcome them.

Now, I'm noticing that in many teams, there's a dedicated time for mind training sessions that's clearly marked in the training calendar. This takes a lot of stress out of scheduling.

Another significant change, particularly for independent sport psychologists, is the rise of the online training modality. Earlier, travel and in-person meetings with athletes were a must. As a trainer, you had to be there with a player. But now, remote training has become fully acceptable after COVID. The younger generation of athletes is comfortable with online training, with the quality of video calls going up. As a trainer, you can be very efficient in doing face-to-face sessions remotely.

Training diaries have become digital. And with chat messengers, it's possible to provide solid support to athletes whenever they need it most. Voice messages, audio recordings of instructions, and relaxation techniques are making training even more effective. You might not be travelling with an athlete for a competition, but they can still call you from the comforts of their room to have a session. During the last Olympic cycle, I trained with an elite shooter completely remotely. None of this training would have been possible without all these technological advancements.

Another big development in the last five years is the use of Athlete Monitoring Systems, where all the training, recovery, assessment, and medical information of the athletes is available. All professionals can collaborate on such platforms. AMS provides up-to-date information about an athlete's training to Sports psychologists. As a result, the time spent in collecting information about ongoing training, skill, and physical assessments have been reduced. More time can be spent on actual training and counselling during sessions.

While things are getting easier on some fronts, challenges still persist with some basics. Convincing players to make fundamental changes in their technique, which are limiting their performance, is the hardest thing to do professionally. Of course, you don't suggest these changes yourself; these usually come from their coaches. And as a team, your role is to help convince the athlete and help them make the necessary changes.

There was a successful Indian boxer who idolized Mohammed Ali and always boxed with his guard down. He was quite successful in India and a few international tournaments from time to time. But he gave away a lot of easy points in important matches due to this. There was no alignment between his personal coach and national coach and, the personal coach was not sure about the change. The player was of a very rigid mindset and didn't believe in mind training. He was deeply committed to his own mental preparation methods, such as listening to bhajans, and was reluctant to explore psychological training techniques. He did not even want to try it. Nothing seemed to convince him, and he ended up stagnating at the same level and did not utilize his huge talent fully.

Some players do make a change. I remember a badminton player who had grown up as a defensive and counter-puncher. Very successful as a junior, but she was not able to go beyond the first or second round in the Super 100s and Super 300s. She started working on her strength and tried to incorporate an attacking game. However, she lost several matches badly and got into a negative phase. When a player is turning their game from a defensive to an offensive style, it is not easy. In real match situations, you often revert to your habits and instincts. There is confusion and second-guessing on important points. In such cases, understanding the gravity of the change and keeping the right expectations is key. You have to bear with the losses for quite some time, and yet stick to the change for a better future. In her case, the counselling helped, and she stuck to the change. She used techniques like self-talk and visualization to practice the new skills regularly.

**Reflection Opportunity:**

Imagine you're working with an athlete who is reluctant to make a critical change in their technique, even though it could significantly improve their performance. The athlete is deeply attached to their current method, and navigating this resistance thoughtfully is crucial.

- If you're already practicing, how would you approach this situation? I'd be interested in hearing what strategies or psychological techniques you might use to help the athlete make the change, while still respecting their attachment to their current style.
- For those aspiring to become sports psychologists, take a moment to think about how you might handle this in the future. What methods could you use to build trust, motivate the athlete, and effectively communicate the need for change?

Though these changes come from the coaches, their expectations of how soon a player would be able to implement new strokes or new serves in matches may or may not be realistic. I worked with a table tennis player whose coach introduced power games introduced new serves to take the game to the next level. This was during a one-month break during a tournament season, and the player was not able to play as per the new plan in the next couple of matches. The coach wanted me to use hypnosis or some new/fancy equipment (he even sent me links to various mind-training equipment and exotic claims about techniques) to program the player's mind to start using the new methods immediately.

Professionally, another difficult thing is to convince players, and particularly coaches, not to make changes for the sake of it, particularly not making changes before matches. This is true in all sports, and particularly true in shooting and archery. When matches come close, players begin to feel the pressure. They become hyper-aware and begin to notice every small detail. Due to increased muscle tension, the body form changes. The quality of training starts to fluctuate. So, they feel like making changes in the gun and end up changing what is already well set. Relaxation training and counselling are very important in these situations. Sometimes coaches might also make last-minute changes, like adjusting the shooter's position or changing the settings on their rifle or pistol one week before the tournament. While there could be technical benefits to these changes, it's important to assess whether a player can adapt to the change. It totally depends on the player, and several players can handle the last-minute changes.

Players and coaches have higher standards of professional conduct from the Sport Psychologists, which is understandable to an extent. It is necessary to infuse confidence in your professional skills through your conduct.

When traveling with the team in informal settings, it's important to remember that you're always being observed. Any innocuous comment may get misinterpreted. It is during the most informal settings that mature conduct is important. It is necessary to avoid talking about players behind their backs. You may quickly lose the trust of all players.

I have always believed that one needs to practice relaxation exercises as a professional and apply them in personal life as well. One good application is interacting with players during the matches, watching them perform, and helping them deal with outcomes requires immense self-control. You can help them only if your own emotions are in control under pressure. This is where developing your own self-talk and practicing visualization of how you are going to conduct yourself in different situations can make a big difference.

One of my fondest memories is the time spent in the field during intense training with athletes— those are the pure moments of absorption.

I believe that it is a very noble profession, one that allows you to be a part of the pursuit of excellence. It feels good to be helping players achieve their goals, being part of the journey, helping them deal with their innermost thoughts and feelings, looking for areas of improvement, coming up with a plan, and training hard.

Like any other profession, there are ups and downs. You'll have to face periods of anxiety, rejection, so you have to be emotionally resilient to cope with these challenges.

I still think the field is in its early stages. There are limitations to our understanding, and a lot more research is required. Sharing of data, observations, and collaborative research is required to advance the field.

# IMPLEMENTATION OF A PSYCHOSOCIAL SPORT PSYCHOLOGY PROGRAMME WITH TRIBAL ATHLETES -

VARADAYINI GORHE

> "*Everything negative—pressure, challenges—is all an opportunity for me to rise.*"
>
> **– Late Kobe Bryant,**
> **Basketball player, Mamba Mentality**

Looking back at the pandemic, I recall how the athletes I worked with used their time, effort, and space productively—reminding me of this quote by Kobe Bryant. One of the opportunities that all the players, whether Olympians or grassroots level athletes, embraced was implementing or even understanding the importance of mental training in their athletic life.

One such opportunity I had as a sport psychologist was to work with several residential athletes who belonged to a tribal region in South

India. When I discovered that I was working with these tribal athletes through remote sessions, I was astounded that they reached out and wanted to transform a period without tournaments into a valuable opportunity. In India, tribes refer to ethnic communities with shared ancestry and cultural traditions, often living away from urban areas. Working with athletes belonging to this background would have been completely different from working with urban athletes who have been brought up in a very different way, with different goals.

The start before the start The sports science team junior from the organisation, who was interested in sports psychology, initiated this conversation. The key areas the Sports scientist wanted me and my team (two sport psychologists in training) to address 'making them mentally stronger', 'disciplined', and 'reducing the anxiety'. To top this, we were in the middle of a world pandemic, and that was the first key challenge. We had to work remotely with the group, all 12-19-year-olds. Hence, I involved the coaches and the performance analyst from the beginning. This alignment ensured that coaches and the sport scientist could integrate basic Psychological Skills Training even in the absence of a sport psychologist.

## Needs Analysis: Pandemic and Beyond

The pandemic itself brought many challenges for athletes. Some faced immense pressure to perform after missing a crucial year in their careers, while others feared the rise of new competitors during the lockdown. Due to a lack of competition, there was a lack of real-time performance feedback.

Some also spoke about the pressure to study in case athletic careers didn't take off.

Apart from the challenges mentioned above, which accelerated due to the pandemic, performance-related challenges were also noted. The most common being haphazard goal-setting, lack of communication between the coaching staff and athletes, and lack of self-belief in their performance.

Belonging to a residential sports academy also meant self-management and family management. All the athletes belonged to a particular tribe and came from financially poor families. Apart from the financial pressures, social and family demands were seen, such as getting the girl child married off quickly, and not giving a lot of importance to education and a sporting career. The only incentive the family got from this initiative was financial stability in caring for their child.

As I closely the collected information, the best way of applying Psychological Skills Training was to start by educating them, in group sessions, on the 5 Cs (Harwood, 2008) model of Commitment, Concentration, Confidence, Control, and Communication.

## 5Cs Educational Sessions Performance Profiling

Given the time frame of 5 months before the first competition after the pandemic, I started with a brief performance profiling for each player with triangulated data acquired from coaches and the support staff. The parameters that were assessed were drawn from the understanding of the coach and support staff (Table 1). This profiling data was collected before we started the educational sessions and right before the competitions. The athletes, coaches, and support staff were asked to rate these parameters on a scale of 1-10, 1 being the lowest.

| **Personal Qualities** | **Technical** | **Physical** | **Psychological** |
|---|---|---|---|
| Discipline & hard work | Skills | Nutrition | Focus |
| Time Management | Techniques | Fitness | Mental Toughness |
| Work Ethics | Sprinting form | Endurance | **Self-Belief/Confidence** |
| Respect towards | Your Start | Speed | **Motivation** |
| **Authorities** | | | |
| Consistency & Dedication | Your End | Flexibility | Determination |
| Respecting your kit | | Coordination | **Ability to remain calm** |
| Humble | | Mobility | Empathy towards opponents |
| | | Power / Strength | Acceptance of Failure |
| | | Agility | Independent Thinking & Decision Making |
| | | Balance | Emotion management |
| | | Sleep and Recovery | **Communication** |

**Table 1: Parameters assessed in 2 phases of the programme**

As I sat and planned the intervention stage, we scheduled a group virtual session once every two weeks. Apart from Communication, each C had two sessions. Additionally, activities were given after every session. One of the sport sports scientists on the field was the point of contact and coordination for implementing this programme and translating the English into the local language for some.

Education Session: Commitment with an introduction to setting goals In this session, the concept of communication was explained in simple terms. The athletes opened up about different ways they saw commitment, right from discipline to commitment to time. Common challenges included a commitment to exercise and rehab when injured, committing to a schedule every day, and committing to a sometimes impossible goal. In the following session, the athletes and coaches were introduced to setting process, performance, and outcome goals.

Education Sessions: Control with an introduction to mood tracking The session started with a game which introduced the athletes to various emotions & moods. The athlete was also asked to speak about tournament situations when they felt a range of emotions- happiness and excitement, irritation and anger, sadness and helplessness. This initiated a dialogue between the coach and the athlete to express moods and emotions, and what causes them. A part of their homework was to list down helpful and unhelpful emotions with a list of situations they face (Table 2). The second homework given to the athletes and staff was to track everyone's mood on a board, every time the athlete comes into training.

Education Sessions: Concentration with an introduction to distraction control. The athletes and coaches were briefed on the difference between multiple and single focus points. Every athlete had to write down the important stimuli of focus pre-race, during and after the race. The coaches gave their viewpoints on how the most common distractions stemmed from other athletes who looked much more confident or wore better running shoes and gear. I did an exercise with the athletes, which helped them note down the pre-, during, and post-race distractions. The athletes were also introduced to the concept of controlling the controllables.

## EMOTION REGULATION

| PRE-RACE SITUATIONS | HELPFUL EMOTIONS | UNHELPFUL EMOTIONS |
|---|---|---|
| A week before the competition | | |
| 2 days before the competition | | |
| The night before the competition | | |
| The morning of the competition | | |
| During warm-up the race | | |
| On the blocks before the race | | |
| | | |

**Table 2: A part of the assigned activity for emotional awareness**

### Education Session: Confidence with an introduction to self-talk

While introducing the athletes to the concept of confidence, every athlete had a different picture of being confident. To define confidence, many athletes focus only on the motivational component, and others on self-belief. An activity that helped them define it for themselves was to write as many words as they think of—in any language—when they think of their confidence.

They also started writing a weekly self-analysis that helped them take account of their strengths and weaknesses. This also helped them gain the actual level of self-awareness along with confidence. Secondly, they were also asked to write about common negative self-talk that they experienced and counter it with positive self-talk.

### Education Session: Communication with an emphasis on assertive communication

Educating coaches on the importance of being assertive was deemed important from the feedback we received from the staff and athletes. Sometimes, cultural differences led to a distance in communication, especially with the younger players and the coaches. More than the players, the coaches, and the support staff were taught the repercussions of passive and aggressive communication. Through role plays and case studies, we helped them understand how assertive communication lies somewhere in between the two. This also helped them clarify the words to be used while communicating assertively.

As these sessions came to a wrap, e-booklets of each session, the notes as well as the homework, were provided to the athletes and the coaches in two languages- English and Hindi. This helped the athletes as well as the coaches prepare thoroughly for matches. Secondly, the performance profile was conducted right before the tournaments to see the difference in the parameters.

## Beyond the basics

After the introductory sessions, some athletes continued to take individual sessions. This was slightly different from the educational sessions, as we focused more on personal challenges. These sessions lasted about 6 months for all the athletes. The on-field sports scientist was of great help in developing and keeping track of the activities done by the athletes.

## Challenges and a critique

While implementing this programme, the most important challenge for me was keeping confidentiality intact during sessions, group or individual.

Since I was working closely with the coaches and most importantly, the sports scientist who was helping me get the homework done, getting the mood tracker up and running, and also getting the athletes set up in the room every week, it got very difficult not to tell this entourage anything less. But while reflecting on this today, it was challenging, but meant that as a sport psychologist, I adapted to the situation and handled it with care.

The second most important challenge was language. Although everyone understood Hindi, translating some words in the local state language was difficult.

Thirdly, cultural differences played an important role while working individually with the athletes. The coaches and I did not take some beliefs and systems very well into account. For example, one family believed performing certain rituals before matches would ward off all the evil from their child. Tackling such issues, especially with the family, which formed a huge part of the athlete's belief system, was challenging. While working with the on-ground coaches, I guided the coach in having a conversation with the mother to help her explore the role of rituals in performance from a broader perspective.

**Reflection corner:**

Have you encountered challenges in implementing psychological interventions across diverse cultural settings? How did you adapt your approach to ensure effectiveness while respecting cultural beliefs and values?

## Key Takeaways

- To conclude this chapter, I have the top five takeaways and protocols to keep in mind while working in a hybrid environment and working with tribal groups of athletes: Sport Psychologists working in a Hybrid Environment Although it is a norm to work from home for most companies
- post-pandemic, sport psychology sessions should never be only online. Unless the client is in another far-off land.
- Online sessions meant observing their body language or audio tone to understand a lot more than verbal communication
- The hybrid model works well because you need to meet the athlete to develop rapport repeatedly.
- Be mindful of giving your full attention during sessions. Avoid distractions like checking your phone, as it can make the client feel unheard. While long conversations may seem repetitive, active listening is essential to maintaining engagement and trust.
- Paperwork and storage of the client's sessions.

# PERFECTIONISM IN SPORT AND ITS MANIFESTATION -

## PARINAAZ IRANI

### Introduction

Practice makes us perfect, a widely celebrated proverb that describes how most kids are taught to work hard in school, sports, or other endeavours. I come from a similar background, and this was one of the unrealistic and rigid (I wasn't willing to change it) beliefs that dominated my years of training in sport. I practiced really hard, set high standards of performance, and enjoyed pushing myself to reach those standards. This made me a good student of the sport and a quick learner as well. Along with sport, it helped me achieve good grades, high-quality work, and appreciation, and slowly that mindset took hold of my overall approach towards any task. I wanted to be the best, and that best came from seeking perfection.

Little did I realise that all my hard work was driven by an unrealistic need to be "flawless"—someone who makes no mistakes and excels in every match she plays. Every bad shot I played at crucial moments was widely criticized by me. I didn't need a coach shouting at me—I had an internal policeman loudly judging my every shot on court. I distinctly remember, even though I was aggressive on the outside, I was scared internally, and I was unsure. Every mistake was eroding my confidence.

Unaware of my own perfectionistic tendencies, funnily, this concept took my interest during my post-graduation in clinical psychology. I enthusiastically developed a questionnaire/psychometric on multidimensional perfectionism and also conducted my master's thesis on the effect of perfectionism on burnout. The more I studied the concept, the more I resonated with it and started realizing those patterns in my behaviour. I started becoming aware of its ill effects on our self-concept in the long run and how it had impacted my confidence, too. Another important realization was how unsatisfied I was with my journey and dreaded how others would view me and my "expertise."

In hindsight, my proudly held 'perfectionistic standards' actually kept me away from performing to my potential, inside and outside sport.

Today, I write this chapter, not only from a place of lived experience, but also because I find many of my clients deal with perfectionism and its negative impact. Many athletes do not even realise how it shows up in their behaviours.

Importantly, perfectionism is both supported and often demanded in sports, as it's believed to drive athletes towards peak performance. Recently, the coach of double Paralympian Avani Lekhara mentioned in his interview that Avani is a perfectionist, which is a *very good attitude.* This is one of the many examples of perfection being celebrated in sport, especially target and precision sports.

Let's first understand what exactly is ***perfectionism?***

Perfectionism is broadly defined as a combination of striving **for unrealistically high standards and overly critical evaluations.**

a) In sport psychology literature today, perfectionism is considered to be a multidimensional trait, with multiple models highlighting different characteristics of perfectionism like concern over mistakes, self-doubt, self-oriented vs other-oriented perfectionism, etc. (Frost et al; 1990; Hewitt & Flett, 2005). One of the commonly used multidimensional models was given by Hewitt and Flett (2005), who described perfectionism as a multi-dimensional concept consisting of 3 dimensions:
b) **Self-oriented perfectionism** -excessive striving and demanding absolute perfection from ONESELF
c) **Other-oriented perfectionism** -demanding perfectionism from OTHERS around us

**Socially prescribed perfectionism** - the perception that others demand perfection from us, so we adopt those standards; in essence, it's internalised perfectionism.

Factor analytical studies have organised these models into a higher-order model with two dimensions of perfectionism: perfectionistic strivings (PS) and perfectionistic concerns (PC) (Hill et al., 2024)

1. **Perfectionistic strivings** refer to self-oriented striving for perfection and setting of very high personal standards of performance
2. **Perfectionistic concerns** refer to concerns over making mistakes, fear of negative social evaluation, feelings of discrepancy between one's expectations and performance, and negative reactions to imperfection (Gotwals et al., 2012, p. 264)

Together, these dimensions highlight how perfectionism is not only about aiming for the stars, but it's combination with a <u>demand</u> for those standards to be achieved and <u>fear</u> of mistakes, which makes it unhealthy and counterproductive (note - the fear could be the fear of mistakes, failure, self-doubts or being judged). Going back to my journey, we can see how I was driven to achieve high standards, but

I also demanded a flawless performance every single time, driven by a fear of failure.

Please note - we use the term perfectionistic rather than perfectionist, because we see it as a trait; something that we may all exhibit to varying levels. So instead of an identity as 'perfectionist,' we use the term 'perfectionistic.'

Research studies have found a negative impact of perfectionistic concerns on athletes' performance and well-being, but the findings on perfectionistic strivings are more complex (read meta-analysis by Hill, Mallinson-Howard & Jowett, 2018)

Another key finding by Hewitt et al. (2003) highlighted how there are individual differences in the demonstration of perfectionism and people may be driven to 'showcase' perfect actions without actually identifying as one.

## Manifestation of Perfectionism

Now that we have an understanding of what perfectionism is, let's see how it actually shows up in our behaviours

**(I'd recommend using these points as a checklist and ticking the points that may resonate with you as a self-assessment or for a client)**

1. **Emotional reactivity** (known as Perfectionistic reactivity) to adversity/loss, which shows up as anger, anxiety, depression, and/or behaviours like avoiding activities, becoming hypercompetitive, getting stuck in repetitive negative thinking (about the past or future); comparison with others
2. **Taking too long on certain tasks/ drills** to ensure that they do them perfectly at the expense of overall growth.
3. **Practice will help me achieve 100% skills,** so I might put in efforts only till I reach that 100% standard

4. **Intolerance of mistakes in others,** which can create friction in their relationships with their team, friends, family, etc.
5. **Identity generalizations,** labelling oneself as a 'failure' based on a poor performance, rather than saying that they failed at a task. This can also be seen as an all-or-nothing mindset- which is an extreme thought process of either being a great player or a failure
6. **Unwilling to seek help,** which could be related to sport or even outside sport
7. **Procrastination**: usually, high standards motivate us in making sustained efforts towards our goals. However, unrealistic standards may stop us from starting because of focusing on the "outcome" of perfection, which can be overwhelming or create fear of mistakes.
8. **Never feeling satisfied:** Constant upward comparison (am I there yet?) with own standards or others, which can leave them feeling unsatisfied. One of my athletes had mentioned how he never feels satisfied with his performance, even though he trains harder than most others
9. **Inability to accept feedback constructively** – perfectionistic individuals may perceive feedback as a threat to their identity rather than being helpful
10. **Risk or change averse-** they would usually tend to avoid a new way of doing things to avoid losing control, despite the need for change
11. **Impatience-perfectionism** as a goal can make athletes become impatient in the journey to those unrealistic standards. They may also expect to excel at skills in the first few attempts. And when this is not achieved, they feel dejected. Individuals with high other-oriented perfectionism would be impatient with their teammates and their mistakes.
12. **Unwilling to take responsibility** in the team so that their poor performance would not be seen negatively

13. **Immoral behaviours** have been shown to be associated with perfectionism in athletes, as they may hold a mindset of "win at any cost"
14. **Excessive self-criticism-perfectionism**, in particular perfectionistic concerns, stems from an underlying fear and feeling of not being enough. This can make us intolerant of mistakes
15. **Focus** on avoiding mistakes rather than aiming for improvement.
16. **Hypervigilant** of others' comments or judgements, or reactions 17.**Overtraining to** attain quick results and to stand out
17. **Lastly, reduced enjoyment,** as we can see, unrealistic standards may make us blind to the enjoyment in the journey. They underestimate the time it would take those standards E.g., you want to clock 10 secs in 100m in the next 2 months, but currently are at 13 secs. This is usually unlikely and would create stress and anxiety with each passing day about attaining that timing, and they could get upset with even one day of missed training.

All of these are examples of how perfectionism might manifest in athletes. As we can see, these behaviours shall not only impact an athlete's ability to perform at their peak, but also negatively impact their self-confidence and self-concept.

## Need for perfectionism in sport?

In the context of sport, most athletes identify as perfectionistic, and their efforts in sport are directed towards attaining the "perfect" score, form, or overall performance. Certain sports demand perfect performances, like diving, synchronized swimming, gymnastics, precision sports, etc.

Flawlessness and perfect performances can make or break their efforts through the years. Also, it's not only about perfect performances but also consists of perfect portrayals to avoid judgments by parents, coaches, selectors, peers, etc. Many of the cricketers I worked with shared how their focus during selections was on looking like the perfect bowler, rather than actually focusing on the task.

At the larger level of the sport and society culture, too, there is a belief in –'Perfection is the other end of effort,' and the more our kids push, the closer they will get to perfecting that shot.' There is no malice in their thought, but the pressure can be quite detrimental for athletes, and they may also become intolerant to mistakes over a period of time. I have had athletes who have driven themselves to overtraining or ended up hating the sport because of the parental/ coach pressure they experienced. They were expected to play their best in every training and performance, and unfortunately also physically abused for mistakes.

This is referred to as the **perfectionism paradox.** It states that despite sports demanding perfection in execution, unhealthy patterns and self-defeating behaviours are often observed in individuals who are focused on attaining perfection.

This continues even though research has indicated the ill-effects of perfectionistic concerns on the performance and well-being of athletes.

> An important question to then ask is what kind of mindsets or beliefs are we letting our athletes develop today?

Before we move to finding solutions, let's reflect on our perfectionistic beliefs and thoughts for 2 minutes. Read the table below and identify 5 perfectionistic thoughts that you may have experienced this week.

**Self- Awareness activity**

**Identify your perfectionistic thoughts in a diary**

Perfectionistic thoughts would usually consist of a "demand" (e.g. have to, should, must) for a standard or imperfection/ flawlessness. Identify 5 perfectionistic thoughts, around sport or outside sport, that you have experienced in the past few days.

1._________________________________________
2._________________________________________
3._________________________________________
4._________________________________________
5._________________________________________

**A possible solution? AN EXCELLENCE MINDSET**

If perfection isn't a "goal" we can set, am I recommending lowering our standards so that the negative impact of perfection can be avoided? Not really, so let's look at an alternative.

One of the athletes that I was working with was a talented 20-year-old cricketer, who played A-level club cricket in Mumbai. When I met him for the first time, he spoke with certainty about his goals, and he was very disciplined and stuck to his routine. But in the initial few sessions, he looked sombre instead of excited. It felt like he carried so much weight on his shoulders and was so scared of not achieving his goals. He disliked any changes in his plans and felt "he had to perform" because time was running out!

Working through his thoughts and beliefs, he started realising the importance of focusing on the 'Process' and not only the outcome, adopting smaller habits that can help him enjoy and appropriately switch off from cricket too. One change I noticed more than anything was that, slowly, a weight was lifted off his shoulders. He looked 20 again, and he had this positivity in his demeanour. He was more focused than before, but also lighter.

As you may have noticed, I didn't immediately focus on the results—whether he got selected further or became the man of the match—as the focus here isn't on results. The aim was to shift his mindset, including his self-talk changing from a result-oriented one ('I have to win') to embracing a process-oriented mindset ('watch the ball' or 'ball to ball'), which would inevitably ensure his success, as he did, in fact, get selected.

**His goal changed from perfection to growth, process, and excellence.** **DEALING WITH PERFECTIONISM**

Before finding an appropriate solution, it is crucial to understand how the perfectionistic tendencies of the athlete are manifesting. The above table might have given you a peek into different thoughts that may come up for you/ your athlete.

There are also standardised perfectionism questionnaires that can be utilised.

E.g., Performance perfectionism scale-sport (Hill et al., 2016), Sport multidimensional perfectionism scale 2 (Gotwals & Dunn, 2009).

**Two other assessment techniques that can be used are:**

1. Draw an image of your "perfect performance," – which can help indicate their expectations and standards. The details mentioned in these drawings have been helpful to understand what is important to the athlete (e.g., being seen as a good player or teammate) and provide the athlete with clarity on how realistic their standards are.
2. Identify the goal of practice/performance- **Is perfection a goal during your practice?** Identifying the goal helps provide

clarity on the client's approach to practice and performance. e.g., demanding perfection in each of her shots, a 12-year-old tennis player was intolerant of any poor shots in practice and also during matches. She kept using only her favourite shots and threw the match away if she started hitting poor shots. Her goal was perfection rather than progress or excellence.

Moving forward, as you have identified your perfectionistic thoughts earlier, let's reflect on them.

| | |
|---|---|
| **1. Rate those thoughts (0-10, 0 being lowest, 10 being highest) on -**<br>**a. Consistent:** How consistent is this thought in your head?<br>b. How **helpful** are these thoughts for me to reach closer to my peak performance?<br>c. How **motivated** does this thought make me feel to practice/ perform? | 1. a.___b._______c._______<br>2. a.___b._______c._______<br>3. a.___b._______c._______<br>4. a.___b._______c._______<br>5. a.___b._______c._______ |
| **2. Triggers**<br>**a. Situations:** Do your perfectionistic thoughts and behaviours occur more often in certain situations or activities?<br>**b. People:** Do you tend to get more perfectionistic around certain types of people? | a. Situations<br>b. People |
| **3. Impact**<br>How do these thoughts impact your mood and performance? | |

Once we are aware of our perfectionistic thoughts and triggers, we can evaluate these thoughts to start building a new mindset which is geared towards EXCELLENCE rather than PERFECTION.

Lastly, in my personal experience as well, self-compassion has been key in working through perfectionistic tendencies, because change takes time and can make us confront our biggest fears of imperfection, uncertainty, and/or criticism. The best way of building self-compassion is by changing the way we speak to ourselves. Instead of saying "Why are you making such silly mistakes?", we can reframe it to "I know you are trying your best, let's keep going." In fact, self-talk has been found to help maintain a positive attitude and consistent temperament in sport (Flemming & Dorsch, 2024), which can be very helpful for individuals with high levels of perfectionism.

## Conclusion

Perfectionism can be a vulnerability for athletes, but with awareness, self-compassion, and a focus on excellence, it can be reframed. Creating a supportive sporting culture—where mistakes are part of growth and excellence is the goal—helps athletes thrive. Parents, coaches, and stakeholders play a crucial role in guiding athletes through clear progress plans and reinforcing that they are more than just their sport.

From a research perspective, understanding the moderating factors of perfectionism (e.g., needs satisfaction, sport, gender) and how perfectionistic standards vary across contexts remains vital. For many athletes, shifting toward flexible standards may feel counterintuitive, requiring patience and emotional regulation support.

Ultimately, while perfectionism may enhance performance, we must ask: does it truly serve an athlete's overall well-being?

# MENTAL TOUGHNESS -

## MUGDHA BAVARE

The term "Mental Toughness" is widely recognized, especially in the field of Sports. It seems to be something not so difficult to achieve at times. However, according to sports psychologists, that's the mantra for success or for reaching one's true potential. Yet, it remains a difficult concept to understand and is often ignored.

My experience as an athlete and then later as a sports psychologist says that the difference between good and great is absolutely very thin. And the most important factor that divides both is how mentally strong and tough an athlete is.

I was a National-level swimmer, winning many championships, and also represented my country in International events. My swimming career spanned from 1984 to 2000. I still remember that as a swimmer, I was lucky to have an extremely good feel of the water (an important ingredient in the world of swimming), due to which technically I was extremely strong along with the fitness (though back then, Sports Science was nearly nothing). This helped me tremendously in picking up the sport quickly, and within a few months of training, I was performing brilliantly at competitions and very quickly came onto the National scene and podium finishes.

However, this early recognition and accolades brought their own pressures and expectations along with it, which started to interfere with my performances, and I did find it extremely difficult to fight those demons and perform.

As I later transitioned into the field of Sports Psychology as a profession, I realised what had actually stopped me from moving to a bigger stage like 'Olympics', which my coaches always had expectations and more so confidence in me that I could do it. Not being mentally tough or having too much performance pressure and expectations attached to it was something that suppressed my capabilities and impacted the performance.

This was an eye-opener for me. While studying Psychology, I found the concepts deeply relatable to my experiences as an athlete. I realized that if applied correctly, psychological theories and techniques could make a significant difference for athletes. This sparked the thought of taking up the field of Sports Psychology and getting into the applied side of it.

What is Mental Toughness?

Mental Toughness is a phenomenon that comes up very often when we talk about sports. We hear people saying, "That athlete was not mentally tough, that's why he crumbled under pressure," or, " It must have taken him immense mental toughness to recover from such a terrible injury." This term is widely used by everyone who is even remotely involved in the sports industry. However, this quite loosely used term is not so simple to break down. Mental Toughness is an umbrella term that encompasses many aspects of resilience. Researchers for a very long time have tried defining Mental Toughness. Mental toughness is strongly related to the level of psychological fortitude and resilience displayed by people in the face of stressful situations, setbacks, and pressure. As a result, this quality enables athletes to perform at their peak, stay on top of their game, and push themselves to new heights.

The four Cs of mental toughness are confidence, challenge, commitment, and control (Clough, Earle, & Sewell, 2002). These were the factors that were very visible in my practice over the past several years. The term Mental Toughness incorporates numerous factors. Below are some of the key ones that define it.

## Control:

Control in sports psychology is an essential ingredient as it helps athletes perform under pressure, maintain consistency, and adapt to challenges during competitions. It is often developed through certain mental training techniques. The focus of my work is initially to make the players understand and identify the thoughts that lead to the experience of emotions and their impact on the behaviour. The link is very subtle, and under pressure, athletes tend to miss out on these important areas.

## Commitment:

Mentally strong people put their all into everything they do and always give their best. However, in my practice, I realised that players are very committed and devoted to working hard; the challenge lies in leveraging this trait to enhance performance. If dedication and commitment are synced in with goal identification and getting a fun element attached to it, then the advantages are twofold.

## Challenge:

Beyond commitment, a mentally tough athlete sees every stressful circumstance as difficult and concentrates on the positive outcomes. It is very crucial that players accept the situation as a challenge and overcome the threat. The competitions, tournaments will bring in the element of pressure to it. However, the athlete needs to learn to turn around this threat by structuring the thought process in a similar manner. The more the players do this and imbibe the habit of it in regular training, the habit will get formed. These habits are helpful in bringing in consistency towards the performance, the very ingredient to performance.

## Confidence:

The term confidence is spoken about by every athlete and coach. However, building it up lies in training in every way. Most of the athletes believe that confidence will automatically come during competitions or performances. The fact is that it requires time to be built, and the only way to do it is through training. Hence, identifying certain situations that may pull down the confidence, having a plan and structure to work on it, and working on certain mental training techniques would surely lead to confidence enhancement over time. And starting this process early in life is always recommended.

In sports, mental strength becomes an important factor to be able to perform to one's full potential. The term mental toughness is used very frequently within the sporting community to describe how good athletes become great athletes. Mentally tough athletes appear confident, resilient, positive, and focused even in the phase of adversity.

Mental toughness is defined as an athlete's ability to endure in the face of challenges, mistakes, and failure. It encompasses a range of mental skills such as confidence, focus, resilience, emotional regulation, motivation, etc. It involves staying positive and focused on the process by blocking distractions even in high-pressure situations. Mental toughness is a skill that requires developing a daily habit of self-reflection and mindset training.

Mental toughness (MT) has been positively linked to success in athletes and has also promoted adaptive mental health functioning, well-being, and incidents of lower stress levels, depression, and an increase in the quality of sleep (Cowden et al., 2019). When evaluating athletes, most non-elite players only mentally train themselves when they're in a negative state of mind. However, implementing mental training into day-to-day life can be beneficial. Higher levels of mental toughness among athletes were associated with better

performance, more progress toward goals, less stress, better coping skills, and more self-reflection.

**Misconceptions/ Myths (in Indian context) -**

Despite the important role of mental toughness in determining success in sports, it is often misunderstood in the realm of Indian context. These misconceptions lead to harmful consequences for the athletes and teams. They not only act as a barrier towards athletes' full potential but also create a culture of stigma, ignorance, and fear around mental training. Here are some common misconceptions about mental toughness in sports -

- Either you are mentally tough or you are not - Although individuals inherently possess different levels of Mental toughness, Mental toughness is a skill like any other that can be developed and improved through training. One can learn to manage their thoughts and emotions in a way that helps them perform at their best.
- Ignoring emotions is a sign of being mentally tough - Being aware of emotions and handling them in a healthy manner are crucial aspects of mental toughness. It helps enhance resilience and motivation, whereas suppressing emotions can lead to detrimental effects. These include burnout, injury, demotivation, low confidence, and focus.

- If you are stressed, you are not mentally tough. Every athlete feels the stress of pressure situations. Mentally tough athletes accept and acknowledge their stress and work towards managing it, which helps them perform better and to their full potential.
- Mental toughness is an inborn talent - Mental toughness is a skill, meaning that it can be learned and improved on. It requires awareness and mental training regularly.
- Mentally tough people never fail - Mentally tough people also experience failure, but what sets them apart is the way they handle themselves in such situations. They find new solutions, seek help, and take extra efforts to prevent further setbacks.
- Mental Toughness training is only for athletes who are facing problems. Mental training can help all athletes improve their performance. When started at a younger age, it holds more potential to mould athletes in a certain way.

## Challenges I faced:

Despite the critical role of mental toughness in sports, my early years of practice were marked by a significant challenge: helping athletes and the entire sporting ecosystem understand and realize what Sports Psychology / Mental Toughness is all about. Back then, in the early 2000s, there was a lack of awareness not only about Sports Psychology but Psychology in general. Visiting a psychologist was considered a stigma.

That was the challenge that I accepted and worked effortlessly first of all to create and spread awareness about what the mind is all about, its functions, and its impact, especially in Sports and performance. Having a postgraduate background in Psychology, helped me tremendously since the basic skills as a psychologist and a therapist were of great use then.

My background in sports and reaching the international level helped me greatly, firstly to connect to the groups where they could actually accept, relate and identify with the kind of life that I had led and my experiences as a sports person. This was a very tough nut to crack, and it took a while. However, soon I was able to establish a good connection and rapport with the players/ athletes.

## Reflections:

After practicing for 25 years, the experiences, growth, and development over time dhave been immense.

### 1. Personal Growth and Learning:

Over more than two decades, the field of sports psychology has evolved leaps and bounds, focusing on individual techniques to embracing holistic approaches that consider mental health, resilience, motivation, and well-being.

### 2. Impact on Athletes:

It is satisfying to see that the work done over the past many years has positively impacted athletes. Over the years, the athletes' psychological well-being, performance, and mindset have improved due to the interventions and techniques used.

### 3. Successes and Challenges:

After decades of practice, the wealth of experiences, both positive and challenging, is something to cherish. There were a lot of successful cases where the interventions led to significant breakthroughs or improved performance. At the same time, there were instances where I did face challenges, such as athletes' resistance to mental coaching, the difficulty of instilling lasting change, or issues related to team dynamics or individual mental health concerns.

### 4. Adapting to Changes in Sports Culture:

Sports culture and societal attitudes towards mental health in sports have shifted over time. Earlier attitudes toward mental health in athletes were once more stigmatized, but over the years, I, as a Sports Psychologist, have seen a more open approach to mental health support, mental training, and techniques.

## Conclusion

Mental toughness is a key ingredient in athletic success, yet it remains widely misunderstood. With the right awareness, training, and mindset, athletes can develop the resilience needed to perform under pressure. As sports psychology continues to evolve, the focus must stay on equipping players with the mental tools to excel—not just in sport, but in life.

# 'YOU WILL FAIL, FAIL BETTER': SPORTING RESILIENCE FOR ADAPTING TO ADVERSITY AND FAILURE -

## DR. SAHEN GUPTA

Let's start with a story. We all know Anil Kumble, India's former test Captain, former Indian coach, and extraordinary leg spinner, famously nicknamed 'Jumbo' for his large size and upright gait. The year is 2002. We are in the fourth test at Antigua. Kumble walks out to bat and gets a rocket on the jaw of Mervyn Dhillon. The physio rushed out it was clear that he had broken his jaw. He went off the field, straight to the hospital to get treatment for the broken jaw. To everyone's surprise, Anil Kumble takes the field again, determined to help his team by returning with his jaw bandaged and 'wired' shut. The doctors advised against it, but Kumble replied, "At least I can bowl. It's not like I need to speak to anyone!" He knew India had to get Brian Lara out, and if anyone could do it, it was him. He bowled

14 consecutive overs, and in a heroic moment, trapped Lara lbw! Even the West Indian players and fans couldn't help but applaud.

The funniest part came after the match, when Kumble was asked the most obvious question, 'why?'. He quipped, "I didn't want to sit around".

The team eventually drew the test match, and Kumble's act of resilience with a bit of stubbornness went into the book of cricket's famous stories. There are many more instances of players being resilient after an adversity, to come back after failure. So let us understand what resilience is, where it comes from, and how it can be developed.

Let's take a quick peek back in time. While resilience is often attributed to Stoic thought, it appears in Eastern philosophy before that. Circa 2nd Century BCE (and earlier), the Mahabharata, specifically the Bhagavad Gita, highlights what it means to be resilient during times of mental turmoil in Krishna's message to Arjuna. Soon after that, Buddhism in roughly the 4th Century BCE built on Vedic philosophy and accepting difficulties as a part of life to then overcoming them by managing self-defeating thoughts was part of the 'Four Noble Truths'. In Western traditions, resilience was then further formalised in ancient Stoic philosophy with Epictetus and Seneca highlighting that resilience was a key part of life, since life was filled with challenges. Later on, it is most commonly attributed to the Roman Emperor and General Marcus Aurelius in the 2nd Century CE, who outlined resilience as something that is a cornerstone of mental discipline that comes from self-control and rational thinking, which helps individuals endure suffering and loss with composure. The word resilience has Latin origins, from the verb 'resilire', which means 'to leap back'. This captures the essence of recovery or rebound after facing adversity. In modern psychology, resilience has evolved to signify the psychological skill in emotional and behavioural domains, symbolizing a person's capacity to "bounce back" from challenges.

## Is my resilience set in stone?

To answer this question, we have to understand how sport psychology has investigated resilience. In the 1970s-90s, resilience was considered to be a trait that was within the individual's personality. The trait approach to resilience views it as a stable and fixed element in the individual's personality. Resilience was deemed to be an inherent part of an athlete's personality, influencing how they consistently approach and try to overcome adversity. Whatever methods you developed in your early years, and then it was fixed for the rest of your life. This way of looking at resilience was derived from Kobasa's (1979) hardiness theory, which had three core traits: 1) control; 2) commitment; 3) challenges. Athletes high in hardiness and high resilience were considered by how they perceived stressful situations as meaningful challenges to be embraced rather than threats. This perspective helps them approach setbacks with a proactive, resilient mindset. In sport, hardiness is seen as a buffer against stress, helping athletes maintain motivation and performance, even under extreme pressure (Gonzalez et al., 2016).

But research in neuropsychology advanced our understanding of brain development; this changed. Neuroplasticity was discovered. Neuroplasticity is the brain's ability to reorganise and form new neural connections.

Neuroscience research showed that resilience to stress comes from how we learn from adversity, which causes actual changes in the prefrontal cortex (PFC), hippocampus, and amygdala. More recent studies have confirmed this, revealing that resilient individuals exhibit adaptive brain activity patterns: for instance, they show higher PFC engagement, which helps regulate emotions and dampen the amygdala's fear response (Ding et al., 2022), and how resilient individuals experience low anxiety because how their brain activates is different compared to low resilience individuals (Gupta & Reddy, 2024).

From the late 1990s to the present, resilience has undergone somewhat of an evolution in how it is studied and how we work as psychologists to enhance resilience. It is called 'ordinary magic' (Masten, 2014) because resilience is a dynamic and learnable element to an individual's life. Resilience is a flexible process rather than a fixed trait, characterized by adaptive adjustments to

changing stressors over time. Unlike trait-based models, this approach views resilience as the result of ongoing interactions between an individual and their environment, influenced by internal and external resources that vary with context.

### An accidental involvement, but a planned continuation

I always say that I got involved in resilience research through a complete accident. But maybe reflecting back, it was not such an accident after all. Growing up, I was always into sports, several of them. In fact, I still play and compete to this day (although the body hurts a lot more every year!). I competed in the tournament circuits in tennis to a pretty high level, and cricket was always there. I joke now that 'I ran out of talent to be a cricketer, and never got the height to be a tennis player'- while true, it does not take away from the fact that I won a lot, lost a lot, and generally enjoyed the fight along the way. I would characterise myself as someone who is an unhappy but contented man after losing if I have given my all. Fast forward a few years, I was doing my undergraduate degree in psychology, and I started working as the student coordinator for a project with adolescents living with HIV. We aimed to use sport and education as a tool to promote life skills and self-sufficiency. I witnessed the magical capacity of people, children really, who were dealt a huge blow in life through no fault of their own, facing the difficulties of life, and the stigma of people without compromise, with dignity and with a smile.

**Still did not connect the dots.**

Six months later, I was about to do my research project and chose resilience as a topic, along with grit (the ability to engage in goal-directed behaviour over a long period). As most people do in their final years of undergraduate studies, I had a tricky time with personal and academic challenges. I held student leadership positions, which came under threat, and I found roadblocks in the pursuit of my ambitions. The studying I did on resilience helped immensely. After all, I was reading the science behind how people responded to adversities- I am thankful I took the leap and started applying some of those myself.

Very soon after, I started my Doctoral studies in cold, wet Glasgow. This was a massive change. It consumed my life, I used to joke that I was dating my Doctorate. It really was a testing time, and just to top it off, COVID and all it brought with it arrived midway. Being a sincere student, I had done my homework. On the particularly long leg of the flight from Dubai to Glasgow (where the airplane was stuck on the tarmac due to a very dramatic sandstorm), I started sketching out a broad research plan. The same research plan would go on to govern my life for the next three years (it still does in some ways). The goal was simple: 1) Understand resilience in sport, because

the studies that advanced it were done in 2012 and 2014; 2) define and clarify how to apply resilience for athletes and high performers; 3) apply resilience as a psychological element that allows both performance and mental health benefits.

## Understanding Sporting Resilience

Professional and semi-professional athletes who engage in sports long-term encounter various failures, adversities, and stressors throughout their careers (Mellalieu et al., 2009). These athletes also face barriers to success, including personal mental health challenges (Papathomas & Lavallee, 2012) and injuries (Podlog & Eklund, 2006). Galli and Gonzalez (2015) correctly observed that "the question is not if an athlete will encounter adversity in sport, but instead, how will they respond when adversity occurs?" (p. 1, italics as in original), implying a resilience to be a function for success in sport.

This is why understanding how resilience works is a key part of supporting athletes as a sport psychologist, a coach, or a parent. As an athlete, this helps you respond to difficult times better.

Before we have resilience, something needs to go wrong. The first condition of resilience is that there will be 'adversity' (i.e., a difficult or unpleasant situation that causes someone to fail). This adversity can exist in isolation, such as a performance failure in the finals, or as an accumulation of events, such as long-term injury, de-selection, poor form throughout some time (Gucciardi et al., 2011). These adversities also range from how serious they are and how linked to life stress they are. For example, having a manageable injury, such as a sprain, would not have a massive impact as negative life stress, but a big injury, such as an ACL, which requires surgery, will be a major life stress.

### The second condition of resilience is what happens after adversity.

Post-adversity, individuals who can leverage their psychological resilience return to their pre-adversity levels of functioning equilibrium through positive adaptation (Fletcher & Sarkar, 2012).

Typically, this involves displaying no negative pathology or mental ill-being (Luthar et al., 2006) and a context-specific positive outcome (Luthar & Cicchetti, 2000). The context-specific nature of this positive adaptation is key. For someone who has had a very difficult run of performance slumps, the adaptation might be showing glimpses of consistent skill application in a pressure match. Obviously we want the perfect outcome of things being as they were, but this rarely happens.

Sporting resilience is defined as a person's ability to evaluate their thoughts, feelings, and actions when facing adversity, allowing them to adapt and maintain prior performance levels (Gupta & McCarthy, 2022). It is learned through interactions with the environment, involving metacognitive, emotional, and behavioural capacities essential for handling diverse sport-related adversities (Mellalieu et al., 2009; Tamminen et al., 2013). The construct is dynamic, adapting to temporal factors such as career stages and life events, demonstrating resilience as an "environmentally adaptable" and "interaction-dominant" process (Fletcher & Sarkar, 2013; Hill et al., 2018). Gupta and McCarthy (2022) developed this understanding of sporting resilience by looking at all the research on the topic in sport psychology to date. Let's look at the table below to understand the components of sporting resilience:

| Component of Sporting Resilience | Meaning | Example | Case Description |
|---|---|---|---|
| Dynamic Nature | Sporting resilience is dynamic, evolving with changes over time, career stages, personal circumstances, and adversity types, commonly characterized as "ups and downs" or "when-what-where." | Fletcher & Sarkar (2016) highlight how an environment providing balanced challenge and support helps in resilience building. | Raj is a hockey player who has always struggled with his family's support of his sport. Once he got funding after doing well in Khelo India, the taunts increased from his extended family, but his father changed and supported him, fully believing that he could do it. This caused a change in his circumstance and improved his immediate home environment. This allows him to draw on this social support to respond resiliently in times of adversity. |

| | | | |
|---|---|---|---|
| Environment tally adaptable | Constant interaction between the individual and the environment allows for adaptable resilience, where resilience is moulded by context and the capacity to adjust to situational demands. | Environmentally adaptive resilience emerges in sports as athletes face unique, evolving challenges (Hill et al., 2018). | Raj carries on and gets selected for his state U-19 team, being a 16-year-old. All of a sudden, he is asked to move out of home and go to the capital city, where the Academy and High-Performance camp is. His family supports him, especially since all costs are covered. The challenges he faces now become<br>a) dealing with a new coaching system;<br>b) dealing with athletes who are competing for spot on the camp.<br>c) dealing with selectors who often hint that he may have to pay if he does not do well;<br>d) sport scientists who introduce different concepts to him; |

| | | | |
|---|---|---|---|
| | | | e) living away from home. He starts working with a sport psychologist (SP), initially scared, but looking at the different environmental demands and how he would have to 'change his resilience pattern.' |
| Interaction-dominant | Resilience develops through interaction, where individuals learn and re-learn by engaging with themselves and with their surroundings, resulting in behavioural adaptations over time. | Interactional learning is prominent in sports due to the majority of time athletes spend in sporting environments. | Raj has spent 6 months in the centre, and he feels that he is getting comfortable with the setup. He has realised how many different parts hockey has if he wants to play for India. The SP has also highlighted how he can leverage the different specialists to become a better athlete. |

| | | | |
|---|---|---|---|
| | | | Raj spent a lot of time with the S&C to understand his body better (he had always had some pain in his left knee after matches), and worked on it. This resulted in the pain getting better, but more importantly, him having better prepared resources to be resilient when he feels the knee flare up. In the middle, he was out with an ankle sprain for a week, and while he felt it was a major adversity, he used the people around him to be resilient during the process of rehab. |

| Transferable | Skills learned in sports resilience, including coping mechanisms, transfer to non-sporting contexts, and vice versa, allowing resilience from experiences like discrimination to reinforce strength in sports. | Fletcher & Sarkar (2016) and Wagstaff et al. (2016) discuss transfer from non-sport experiences (e.g., overcoming discrimination) as critical in developing sporting resilience. | As April came, Raj was put into a school as well. He had not gone to school for 6 months after leaving home midway, only studying with the tutor in the academy.<br>But joining the new school was a big stressor. He started struggling almost immediately because it was an ICSE board school, with a lot of study pressure. But after the first month, he started using the same strategy he used with his S&C and SPs to get better at hockey. He started talking to his class teacher and coming during recess to plan his study session and deal with the adversity |
|---|---|---|---|

| Combination of Metacognition-Emotion-Behaviour | Resilience is a combination of how we cognitively think about a situation, how we emotionally cope with it, and how we behaviourally respond to it. Being resilient means wc engage in this triple-process every time we engage with adversity. | Individuals combined different elements of their protective resources in a 'uniquely their resilience' response (Gupta & McCarthy, 2022). | Over the years, Raj has figured out how he can deal with failure and difficult stuff i.e., his resilience pattern. He has been using a reflective diary of 'What can I do? How can I solve this?' (cognitive). Then, using breathing techniques taught by the SP to control anxious feelings (emotion). He also used behavioural calendaring to deal with planning responses to stressful and difficult-to-solve situations (behavioural) |
|---|---|---|---|

## How does an athlete become resilient to adversity?

One thing that we have to understand is that there is no constant level of 'resilient' ability. Much like agility, strength, and recovery from a physical perspective, resilience from a psychological standpoint differs and fluctuates. You also have to train for it. Training for it leverages the psychological resources that you use when times get tough. These resources are collectively called the 'biopsychosocial protective filter'. The protective filter is shaped by biopsychosocial elements such as environmental support, optimism, self-regulation, and a sense of meaning, which dilute the impact of adversity. For instance, an injured athlete with strong protective resources adapts more positively than one lacking such support. However, resilience does not eliminate all negative consequences post-adversity. Instead, it is the capacity to adapt despite these challenges (Gupta & McCarthy, 2021; 2022). Just like a strong shield protects you, a strong resilience protective filter shields you from the negative impact of adversity and allows the athlete to recover. A strong protective filter reduces the impact of adversity, resulting in "minimal impact resilience" (Bonanno and Diminich, 2013, p.380). However, when the adversity is too intense, it may overwhelm the filter, leading to a temporary disruption in the individual's normal functioning and performance. This marks the start of an emergent resilience trajectory, which unfolds in four stages:

1. Disruption: Adversity disrupts the individual's daily routine and equilibrium.
2. Depletion: Personal resources are strained as the adversity exceeds the protective filter's capacity.
3. Learning: Through self-reflection, the individual develops new protective resources and strengthens existing ones.
4. Rebound: With these newly acquired resources, the individual adapts positively to adversity, achieving growth and resilience.

### Challenges to develop resilience during challenging times

Over the years, I have done a lot of research working with athletes, coaches, and sports science teams around the world to understand resilience. Most of it has been formally published research, while the rest, informal. I trace a key learning back to a coach who had the perfect blend of old-school strictness and modern sport science openness. I remember him saying, "Sahen- this work is fantastic. There will be one problem though…". I was curious. I asked him, "What? Tell me, I am always trying to improve this". He laughed and went, "That's the problem, you will want to improve. Athletes will want to improve. Few prepare and plan to enable themselves to improve".

If you think deeply about human nature in the context of fast-paced sports lives, it is very true. Athletes often go through the motions in the training phase of it (which constitutes 90% of the time in sport) and overthink the competition phase of sport. The coach was right- I found it to be a struggle to help athletes plan and develop resilience, thought patterns, and behavioural responses. Most did not understand it. Resilience is developed through the

**A-R-C step (Gupta & McCarthy, 2024):**

- Step 1: Antecedents (A) – Prior knowledge gained through interactions with coaches, players, sport psychologists, life events, and various environments. This active learning process requires effort and pre-planning.
- Step 2: Resilience Response (R) – The initial application of learned resilience. Different adversities demand different strategies, and this response acts as the "engine" that drives the athlete forward rather than succumbing to challenges.
- Step 3: Consequence (C) – The outcome of A-R. Adversity may appear in isolated situations, but patterns emerge in responses. This step helps refine future resilience strategies by identifying what works.

This seems quite taxing on the individual. Fundamentally, the process to become resilient is kind of taxing because it demands a lot of preparatory work. That is something athletes are often unwilling to give time for. This is because of two reasons. First: hindsight bias makes them feel that they dealt with it in an 'okay' manner without all the extra mental skills work, and therefore, it will be fine the next time it happens. But athletes always forget the stress and lack of optimal performance in those times. Second, they are in a reactive state. This means that they are usually not proactive about developing their resilience. But they would like to be reactively resilient during a pressure moment in a match, or when they are carrying an injury.

This is nearly impossible to achieve. After all, you cannot make food if you don't get the ingredients.

### Reflection Section

- Thinking about the difficult things that you have attempted in your life, how many have you failed at? (Pick a percentage). How many did you adapt positively to?
- List out the top 3 things that you 'did' in that moment
- Where and when did you learn to do these things that helped? Have they changed over time?
- Now reflect on all three questions

Find out if there are any patterns. That would be how you 'find your resilience.'

## Note from Maana Patel

Growing up, whenever I felt overwhelmed or struggled with my emotions, I often heard people say, "You're not mental; you don't need a psychologist. You'll be fine. This tough phase will pass." Seeking help from a sports psychologist was almost taboo in my surroundings, and the idea of working on mental strength beyond just "toughening up" wasn't widely accepted. But that didn't stop me from seeking the support I knew I needed.

I firmly believe that sports psychologists are an integral part of an athlete's team, not just for performance enhancement but for overall mental well-being. The journey of an athlete is filled with extreme highs and lows, and even the strongest minds need support, guidance, and grounding. High-performance sports demand resilience, but mental toughness alone is not always enough to sustain and thrive in such an environment. Looking after your mental health is just as important as physical training.

In elite sports, athletes are often treated like machines—built to perform, deliver results, and push limits. We get so caught up in training, competition, and expectations that we sometimes forget that we are human first. The pressure to constantly perform at our peak can take a toll, making it easy to lose sight of our own well-being. I was fortunate to have Dr. Chaitanya as my sports psychologist, someone who saw Maana not just as an athlete but as a person. Having that support system allowed me to grow and improve holistically because I knew that my struggles, emotions, and mental state were being acknowledged and cared for. Ultimately, for her, the real victory was that I was a happy person first. A happy person is a successful athlete for sure.

That being said, sports psychologists are not here to mollycoddle or offer blind sympathy. Dr. Chaitanya never sugar-coated things for me. Instead, she made an effort to truly understand me, the challenges I faced, and the situations I'd find myself in. During my toughest moments, she helped me still my mind, block out external noise so I could make rational decisions that were in my best interest. My sessions with Dr. Chaitanya gave me fresh perspectives and strategies to navigate the complexities of elite sports without losing my sense of self.

Sports psychologists play a pivotal role in an athlete's performance and longevity in the sport. If integrated well into the system by coaches, they can make a tremendous difference. Unfortunately, not all coaches are open to embracing sports psychology, and many still undervalue its role in an athlete's development. However, I truly believe that Indian sports can progress significantly if all stakeholders, i.e., athletes, coaches, and sports psychologists, align and recognise the importance of mental well-being. The evolution of sports is not just about improving physical training techniques but also about fostering a culture where mental health is prioritised just as much as physical fitness. Only then can we create a sustainable, high-performance sporting environment where athletes are empowered to reach their full potential, both on and off the field.

**About Maana**

Maana Patel is an elite Indian backstroke swimmer from Ahmedabad, Gujarat, renowned for breaking national records and earning multiple national and international titles. At just 13, she set a new record in the 200m backstroke at the Junior National Aquatics Championship, marking the start of her impressive career. Maana has since secured 32 international medals, 99 national medals, and 31 national records, including golds at the South Asian Games and the Senior National Aquatic Championships. As a member of the Olympic Gold Quest since 2015, she continues to inspire athletes worldwide with her unwavering dedication and remarkable achievements in the pool.

## Note from Manisha Ramadass

Sports psychology has made a significant impact on my performance and mindset as a badminton player. Before I began working with a sports psychologist, I struggled with impatience and often found myself getting nervous and frustrated during matches. When I made silly errors, I would dwell on them instead of focusing on the next point, which affected my overall performance. Since beginning these sessions, I've noticed many positive changes in myself. My psychologist has introduced me to various exercises tailored for specific situations, which have helped me manage my emotions more effectively while playing. For instance, I've learned techniques to reframe my thoughts when I make mistakes, allowing me to quickly shift my focus back to the game instead of getting stuck in a negative loop. Additionally, practicing meditation has allowed me to maintain focus and stay calm under pressure. This practice has been particularly beneficial during crucial points in matches, where maintaining composure is essential. Now, I'm able to regulate my emotions better during matches, which has improved not just my performance, but also how much I enjoy the sport. Overall, sports psychology has not only enhanced my performance but also transformed my approach to the sport, making it a more fulfilling experience.

**About Manisha**

Manisha Ramdass is an accomplished Indian para-badminton player known for her outstanding achievements in international competitions. From Thiruvallur, Tamil Nadu, Manisha quickly rose to the top of the SU5 category after her international debut in 2022, reaching world number 1. She has won multiple gold, silver, and bronze medals at the World Championships and earned three bronze medals at the Asian Para Games. Manisha also secured a bronze medal at the 2024 Paris Paralympics, cementing her place among the best in the sport. In 2022 alone, she won 11 gold and 5 bronze medals and was named BWF Female Para Badminton Player of the Year. Supported by Olympic Gold Quest, Manisha continues to inspire athletes and lead the way for future stars in para-badminton.

SECTION II

# WELL-BEING AND PRACTITIONER AWARENESS

*"Self-care is not a luxury, it's a necessity."*

**– Brené Brown**

# NURTURING THE NURTURERS -

## KEERTHANA SWAMINATHAN

The field of sports psychology, where the complexities of the human psyche meet the rigor of sporting competition, demands a deep understanding of resilience, mental fortitude, and human connection. Our work as sports psychologists requires us to be intimately involved in the lives of our athletes, often acting as their confidants, motivators, and mental strategists. While incredibly fulfilling, this role is also immensely demanding. We help athletes navigate their highest peaks and lowest valleys, pushing them to confront fears, self-doubt, and failures—all while often neglecting our own needs.

In a profession where resilience is often glorified, the act of prioritizing self-care can feel counterintuitive. However, the work we do with athletes is a direct reflection of our inner well-being. Susan David, a leading researcher on emotional agility, emphasizes that "we need to make room in our lives for our emotions rather than suppressing them," a principle that resonates deeply in a field where suppressing one's own struggles is often the norm. This chapter seeks to shed light on the essential practice of self-care in sports psychology, drawing from personal experiences, academic research, and time-tested strategies to create a guide for sustainable practice.

## The Unique Demands of Sports Psychology

Sports psychology extends beyond conventional boundaries. Unlike traditional therapy, our work is dynamic and often conducted outside the typical office setting. We travel with athletes, witness their successes, and support them during their defeats, which requires a unique blend of adaptability and mental resilience. Research shows that chronic exposure to high-stress situations can lead to symptoms of compassion fatigue and burnout, particularly in helping professions (Figley, 2002). In sports psychology, the lines between personal and professional life can blur easily, leading us to absorb the pressures our clients face.

I remember a particular incident with an elite swimmer who had just missed out on a key competition due to illness. After months of training and preparation, the disappointment was palpable, and she turned to me at that moment for reassurance. While helping her process this setback, I felt an unexpected weight settle in my own chest—a sign of empathy fatigue that I initially dismissed. However, over time, I realized that suppressing these responses only heightened my stress. Research supports this phenomenon; studies on emotional contagion, the phenomenon where individuals unconsciously "catch" or mimic the emotions and expressions of others, leading to shared emotional experiences, suggest that exposure to another's emotions can directly impact our own emotional states, which over time can lead to accumulated stress (Hatfield, Cacioppo, & Rapson, 1994).

This constant emotional involvement can leave sports psychologists feeling depleted, yet the societal expectations around self-sacrifice in helping professions can make it difficult to prioritize our own needs. During COVID-19, I recall a time when, due to the increased awareness and demand for sports psychologists, I had to conduct nine sessions back-to-back. I was so exhausted by the end that I fainted as soon as I completed the sessions. That was when I learned and truly understood the importance of taking care of myself. There are times when we just want to help as many people as possible, but it's crucial to remember and respect the "as much as possible" part. If we don't prioritize our own well-being, the work we do won't be sustainable in the long run. As Brené Brown, a researcher on vulnerability and courage, writes, "Daring to set boundaries is about having the courage to love ourselves, even when we risk disappointing others." For sports psychologists, setting these boundaries requires redefining our relationship with self-care—viewing it not as a luxury, but as a necessity to maintain the resilience required in our work.

In India, family holds a central place in our lives and decisions. The idea of balancing personal and professional roles, especially for women, is deeply rooted in cultural expectations. As a sports psychologist, I've often encountered the unique challenge of navigating this balance, both personally and in conversations with others.

I vividly remember a parent of an aspiring sports psychologist once asking about my schedule and the typical demands of this career. With genuine concern, he expressed that he wanted his daughter to settle down, get married, and prioritize family over the frequent travel and unpredictable hours that often come with the profession. This interaction stayed with me, as it highlighted the societal pressures many of us face, even while pursuing our passion for nurturing others.

Nurturing the nurturer is not just about strategies for self-care; it's also a reflection on the challenges that come with being in a profession centred around the well-being of others—balancing cultural expectations, societal perceptions, and the demanding nature of the job. Through this lens, we explore what it truly means to nurture the nurturer.

## The Science of Self-Care and Psychological Resilience

Psychological resilience is not simply a trait; it's a skill that can be cultivated through intentional practices. Research by Luthar, Cicchetti, and Becker (2000) highlights the importance of protective factors, such as social support, self-care routines, and reflective practices, in building resilience and preventing burnout in high-stress professions. This underscores the importance of establishing a structured self-care regimen for those in sports psychology, a profession marked by both high emotional demand and a responsibility to support others.

**Setting Boundaries:** Establishing clear boundaries is an essential practice in managing emotional fatigue and fostering resilience. Susan David's work on emotional agility emphasizes the value of recognizing and accepting our own emotional limits rather than pushing them in pursuit of "endurance" or resilience. In one study, researchers found that professionals who practice self-compassion—setting boundaries, taking breaks, and seeking support—report significantly lower levels of burnout compared to those who don't (Neff & Germer, 2013). In my practice, I began setting time limits on after-hours communication with athletes, a boundary that not only protected my time but also modelled a balanced approach to mental health for my clients.

**Supervision as Self-Care:** Supervision offers a structured and confidential space for sports psychologists to reflect on cases, receive guidance, and develop coping strategies. It helps process emotional and ethical dilemmas that arise in high-performance settings, reinforcing professional boundaries while preventing burnout. Regular supervision allows psychologists to discuss challenging cases, gain perspective, and address self-doubt that may emerge when working with difficult clients or sceptical stakeholders. It also fosters accountability, ensuring psychologists adhere to ethical best practices while refining their decision-making skills. Furthermore, supervision helps establish a sustainable work-life balance by encouraging reflective practice and setting realistic professional boundaries, ultimately enhancing longevity in the field.

Therapy: Despite advocating for mental well-being, sports psychologists often struggle to prioritize their own. Therapy provides a confidential and supportive space for them to manage personal stress, process emotional residue from client interactions, and address underlying triggers that may influence their work. Therapy enhances self-awareness, emotional regulation, and resilience, helping psychologists navigate the pressure of working with elite athletes and high-performance teams. It also offers an opportunity to prevent burnout by fostering self-compassion, helping psychologists manage perfectionist tendencies, and reinforcing healthy coping strategies. Engaging in therapy proactively, rather than as a reactive measure, allows psychologists to sustain their effectiveness while maintaining personal well-being.

**Peer Supervision and Emotional Support:** The concept of peer supervision has become a cornerstone of mental health fields, providing a structured space for professionals to share experiences, seek advice, and process their own emotions. Studies have shown that peer supervision helps reduce feelings of isolation and provides emotional support, enhancing resilience among helping professionals (Morrissette, 2001). In my career, engaging in peer supervision with colleagues has offered me a vital sense of community, allowing me to process challenging cases and receive emotional validation.

This support network has been invaluable, particularly during high-stress periods.

**Mindfulness and Meditation:** Integrating mindfulness practices, such as meditation, into daily routines can have profound effects on mental clarity and emotional stability. Research on mindfulness-based stress reduction (MBSR) shows that mindfulness practices can reduce stress, improve focus, and enhance emotional regulation, making it a valuable tool for sports psychologists (Kabat-Zinn, 1990). Personally, beginning each day with a 15-minute meditation has allowed me to start my work with a centred mind and a sense of inner calm. Studies on the effects of mindfulness on empathy suggest that regular mindfulness practices can increase emotional resilience by reducing susceptibility to emotional contagion (Shapiro, Schwartz, & Bonner, 1998).

**Practical Self-Care Strategies for Sports Psychologists**

1. **Develop a Morning Ritual:** Establishing a grounding morning routine can set the tone for the day. For me, starting with a combination of meditation, stretching, and brief journaling has helped reinforce a sense of calm and purpose. Julia Cameron, in her book *The Artist's Way*, advocates for morning pages as a form of daily mental decluttering, which is particularly useful for practitioners who manage high emotional loads. By jotting down thoughts each morning, I'm able to process and release any lingering anxieties, creating space for focus.

2. **Create Physical Boundaries:** A structured workspace that is distinct from personal space can reinforce the separation between work and home life. This can be especially challenging for sports psychologists who travel frequently. When I'm on the road, I set up a designated workspace in my hotel room and establish "office hours," signalling to myself that outside of these hours, I am off-duty. Research supports that establishing physical boundaries can help in reducing work-related stress and improving mental clarity (Schieman & Glavin, 2008).

3. **Reflective Journaling and Self-Compassion Exercises:** Practicing self-compassion and reflecting on one's experiences

through journaling can help in processing emotions constructively. Neff and Germer's (2013) research on self-compassion training indicates that these practices reduce self-criticism and promote psychological well-being, especially in professions with high emotional labour. I've found that dedicating a few minutes each evening to journaling about my day and practicing self-compassion exercises helps in managing residual stress and fosters a sense of gratitude.

4. **Mindfulness and Emotional Agility Training:** As sports psychologists, we often encourage athletes to focus on what they can control and let go of external outcomes. Practicing mindfulness and emotional agility within our own lives is equally important. Susan David's work on emotional agility underscores the importance of recognizing our emotions without being dominated by them. Incorporating mindfulness exercises into daily routines can build resilience by promoting awareness and acceptance of our own internal experiences, thus enhancing our ability to manage stress.

5. **Regular Physical Activity and Recreation:** Physical activity is often framed as a stress-relief strategy, yet it holds additional value for sports psychologists by allowing us to connect to the physical experiences we encourage in our athletes. Engaging in regular exercise provides not only the physiological benefits of stress reduction but also serves as a reminder of the mind-body connection that we aim to instil in our clients.

6. **Cultivate a Supportive Community:** Surrounding oneself with like-minded individuals who understand the unique demands of sports psychology is essential. Research supports that social support serves as a buffer against burnout and enhances resilience in high-stress professions (Taylor, 2011). For example, I joined a local community of sports psychologists who meet regularly

to discuss cases, share resources, and provide mutual support, which has been instrumental in maintaining a sense of connection and reducing isolation.

## Embracing Self-Care as an Act of Professional Responsibility

As sports psychologists, we often champion resilience and self-compassion among athletes. Yet, embodying these values in our own lives can be challenging. The work we do in sports psychology requires emotional endurance, a trait that is only sustainable through committed self-care practices. By prioritizing our well-being, we not only improve our personal lives but also enhance our effectiveness as practitioners, modelling balanced mental health for our clients.

Self-care is an ongoing process, not a fixed state. Our needs will evolve with the demands of our careers, and adapting our self-care practices accordingly is key. We can only sustain our work if we take care of ourselves first. As Brené Brown puts it, “You can’t serve from an empty vessel.” This sentiment encapsulates the ethos of self-care in sports psychology—it is through filling our own vessels that we can offer the best support to those we serve.

## Exercises / Reflective Activities

These exercises are designed to help you reflect on your self-care practices and identify ways to create sustainable habits that support your well-being. Whether you’re a sports psychologist, coach, or athlete, taking time to nurture yourself is crucial—not only for your own health but also for those who rely on your strength and guidance.

## Identify Your Self-Care Gaps

Reflect on your current self-care practices. Are there areas in your life where you feel constantly drained or unsupported? List three specific challenges you face in maintaining self-care. Then, brainstorm realistic ways to address each of these challenges. Consider both practical adjustments (such as finding time for a break) and emotional needs (such as finding support from others).

Revisiting this exercise regularly can help you stay proactive in supporting your own well-being.

## Boundary-Setting Practice

Spend 15 minutes thinking about situations where your personal boundaries often get tested—whether it's taking calls after hours, handling high-pressure requests, or sacrificing personal time. List these scenarios, and next to each, write what an ideal boundary would look like for you. Then, think of gentle, assertive ways you could communicate these boundaries with others, whether it's colleagues, clients, or family members. Learning to set boundaries not only protects your well-being but also makes you more effective in your role.

## Mindfulness Meditation Practice

To support resilience and focus, try a daily mindfulness practice. Set aside 5 minutes each day to focus on your breathing, letting go of any stress or tension that arises. This can be as simple as sitting quietly, noticing your breath, and allowing any thoughts to pass without judgment. After a week, reflect on the effects: Are you noticing more patience or energy? Greater calm? Mindfulness can bring a sense of balance and clarity, making it easier to navigate the demands of your role.

## Daily Journaling Exercise

Inspired by Julia Cameron's *The Artist's Way* (2002), try journaling freely for just 5 minutes a day. Write about whatever comes to mind—thoughts, emotions, frustrations, or inspirations. This exercise is especially helpful for processing stress or challenging emotions. After a month, review your entries to see if you notice any recurring themes or changes in perspective.

Journaling can provide clarity, emotional release, and valuable insights about your journey.

## Connecting with Peers

Having a support network can be invaluable. Identify two or three colleagues or peers you trust, and commit to connecting with them at least once a month. These check-ins offer a space to share challenges, exchange strategies, and provide mutual encouragement. Reflect on how these conversations impact your own sense of well-being. Whether you're a psychologist, coach, or athlete, a strong peer network can alleviate feelings of isolation and offer fresh perspectives on the demands of your role.

By integrating these self-care practices into your routine, you'll find it easier to stay balanced and resilient. Remember, taking time to nurture yourself is not a luxury—it's essential for performing at your best and being able to support others effectively.

# GENDER INCLUSIVITY IN SPORT -

GAURI SHRINGARPURE AND AMALINA

## INTRODUCTION

For any hands that have picked up this book, or any eyes that are scanning these pages, there is likely some personal connection, small or big, remote or intimate, with sports. Whatever the connection, there is no denying the larger meaning sports hold for us. While the roots of "sport" meant an activity for personal amusement and enjoyment, it has, over the years, evolved to represent some powerful human values like fairness, respect, teamwork, and perseverance.

Unfortunately, along with these values came the rules around who can participate in sport and who cannot. Gender creeped into the mix, and historically, sport became the closely guarded activity of men. Interest in sport or playing a sport gradually became socially equated with masculinity. Women in sport were a rarity, and those who dared to step into the sports arena were considered an oddity. Equality between men and women in sport was fiction for the longest time, and still is.

Although in some sports there may be pay uniformity, lesser opportunities to play professionally, limited endorsements, and reluctant societal acceptance, all ensure that the gap is kept intact.

While the world of sport struggles to bring justice from the standpoint of the gender binary (man-woman framework), it is equally, if not more, important to ask ourselves the question - What about genders beyond the binary? Where does modern sport stand when it comes to those of us who identify as trans, non-binary, or gender-diverse persons with varied gender identities?

These are important questions, and we are optimistic in thinking that if you have come this far in the chapter, you are invested in thinking and possibly acting on addressing this gap in some way.

## ROADMAP FOR THE JOURNEY OF GENDER INCLUSIVITY IN SPORTS

Any journey begins with an intention. The intention could be something deeply personal, like growth or self-exploration, or it could be something more tangible, like experiencing a place or sourcing artefacts specific to the place.

Intention, therefore, is the fuel of the journey. In our journey towards inclusion in sports, our intention to make sports what it truly stands for, is the power we will run on.

How well we take this journey and to the degree of accuracy with which we achieve what we set out to do, has a lot to do with what attitude and values we carry with us all through. How we are BEING in this process matters. BEING is what we are: our values and mindset. Parallelly, what we are DOING will set our intention into motion. Hence, DOING is how we get going with our intention: Knowledge and Skills. This combination of BEING + DOING is the recipe for embarking on this path, where the destination of gender inclusivity would be reached sooner or later.

## ROADMAP FOR GENDER INCLUSIVITY IN SPORTS

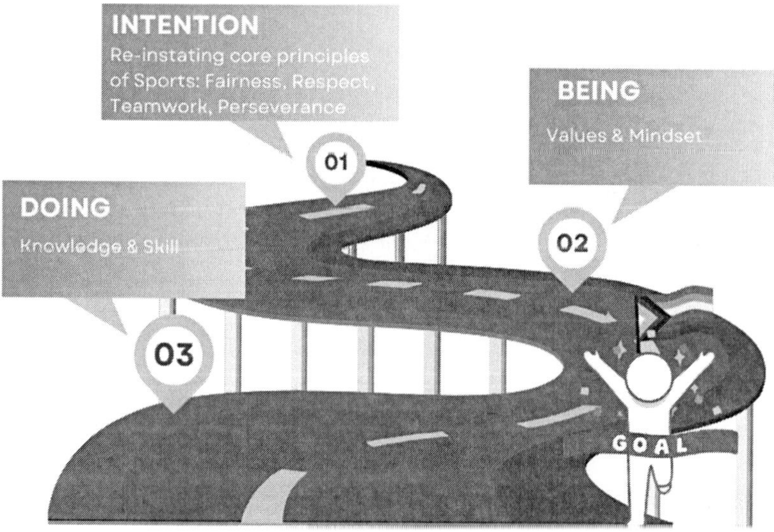


## BEING

Values and attitudes we hold about anything that matters to us are significantly shaped by our perspectives. Understanding the larger systemic context, correlating it with societal norms, and analysing the impact of these on how sports are viewed will help us understand where the "Being" gap lies. Let us do a reflective exercise to build our perspective around Sports and its relationship with Gender.

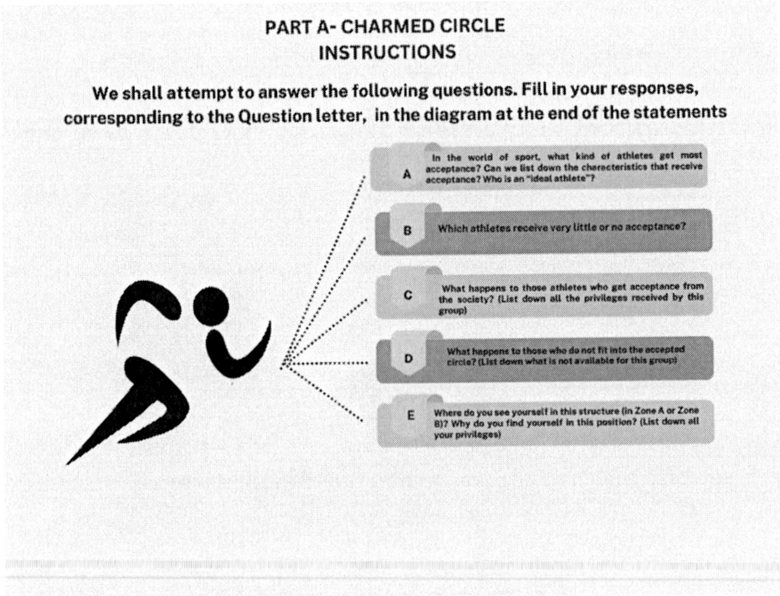


A. In the world of sport, what kind of athletes get the most acceptance? Can we list down the characteristics that receive acceptance? Who is an "ideal athlete"?
B. Which athletes receive very little or no acceptance?

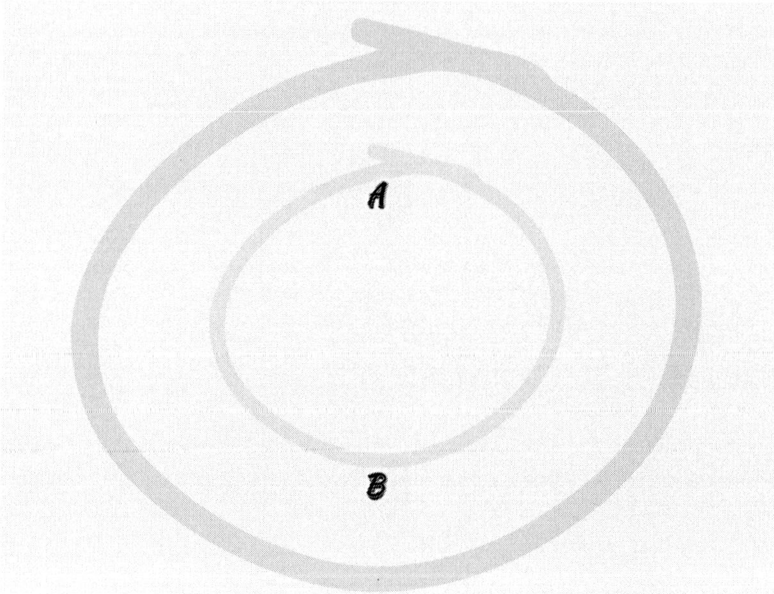


**FIGURE 1**

C. What happens to those athletes who get acceptance from society? (List down all the privileges received by this group)
D. What happens to those who do not fit into the accepted circle? (List down what is not available for this group)

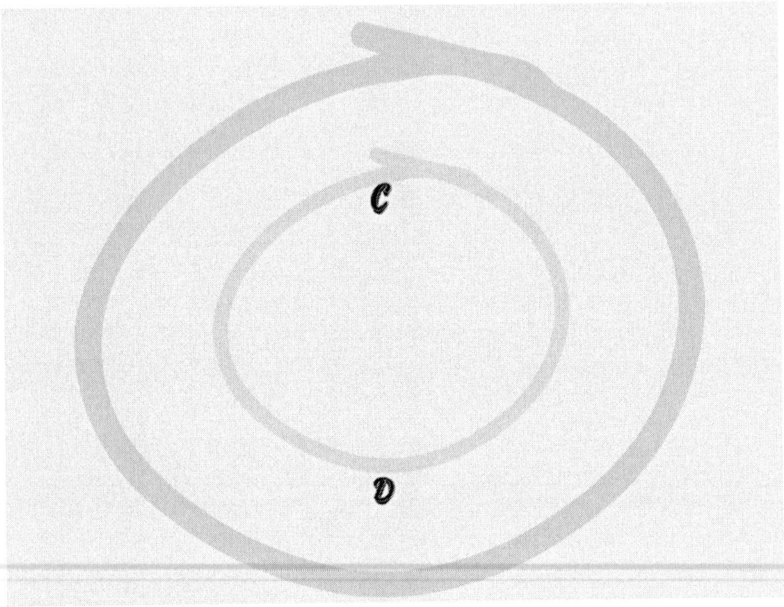


**FIGURE 2**

E. Where do you see yourself in this structure (in Zone A or Zone B)? Why do YOU find yourself in this position? (List down all your privileges) Place an X to mark your position in Figure 1.

E

**FIGURE 3**

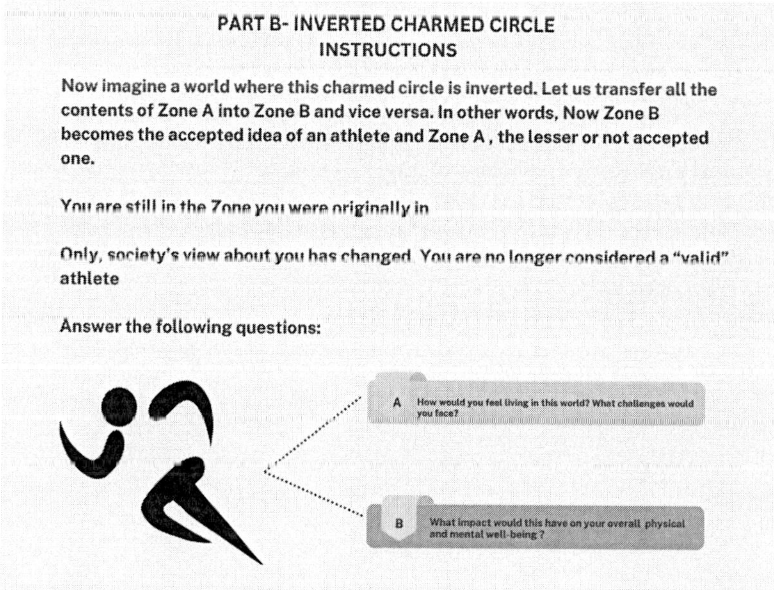
PART B- INVERTED CHARMED CIRCLE
INSTRUCTIONS
Now imagine a world where this charmed circle is inverted. Let us transfer all the contents of Zone A into Zone B and vice versa. In other words, Now Zone B becomes the accepted idea of an athlete and Zone A , the lesser or not accepted one.
You are still in the Zone you were originally in
Only, society's view about you has changed. You are no longer considered a "valid" athlete
Answer the following questions:
A
How would you feel living in this world? What challenges would you face?
B
What impact would this have on your overall physical and mental well-being ?

Some very stark facts come to light when we look at our responses to these exercises. Sports is often structured around a binary gender system, typically recognizing only two genders: male and female. Strict regulations define who is considered "fit" to compete in these categories, excluding those who do not conform to these norms. As a result, gender-nonconforming athletes frequently face barriers to participation or experience discriminatory treatment. This exclusionary treatment can range from not allowing them to participate in organised professional sports to downright physical and emotional bullying.

This exclusion and the queerphobic and transphobic attitude, especially from sports authorities, harm the mental health and performance of these individuals. For queer, trans, and gender-diverse people, sports can become yet another place where they face discrimination and harassment.

Understanding these challenges means recognizing the privileges of fitting into traditional gender norms and finding ways to make sports more inclusive.

In Part B of this exercise, it becomes clear that as the world changes around us and the societal gaze becomes hostile and unaccepting towards us, our experience changes. Hence, the negative treatment some athletes face is not a result of who they are, but rather a consequence of how societal norms define and enforce expectations of gender in sports.

These reflections can form a good starting point to look closely at our own values and mindsets regarding gender inclusivity.

**VALUES AND MINDSET THAT PROMOTE GENDER INCLUSIVITY IN SPORT**

| |
|---|
| FAIRNESS IN OPPORTUNITIES |
| RESPECT FOR DIVERSE IDENTITIES |
| REJOICING IN DIVERSITY |
| HAVING A COLLABORATIVE STANCE |

## DOING

Quite often, the question arises: We have the intention and we have the required values and mindset, but what ACTION do we take? What do we DO? We do commend the eagerness to take charge and swing into action to get closer to our goal of gender inclusivity. However, Action without Knowledge is like driving on unfamiliar roads without a GPS- one would probably get lost! Our quest for Gender inclusivity in sports would be utterly rudderless if we were only armed with tools and techniques without really understanding or knowing the subject.

For a fragile sapling to grow into a blossoming, glorious plant, it needs good soil, enough sunlight, adequate water, and the care of a skilled gardener.

Similarly, athletes require a supportive environment to grow and succeed. In addition to their own talent and dedication, they need a robust and supportive ecosystem to thrive. For GNC athletes, this support becomes critical not just because they can thrive, but also because they can survive as athletes.

As persons who actively work with the LGBTQIA+ community, we have put together a set of practical guidelines as ready reckoner for three important support pillars of GNC athletes: Parents, Coaches, and Sports psychologists.

| **SPORTS PSYCHOLOGISTS** | |
|---|---|
| **WHY SPORTS PSYCHOLOGISTS?**<br><br>**In the world we live in, GNC athletes experience a great deal of discrimination, harassment, and bullying, which significantly impacts their mental health. Feelings of unworthiness, low self-confidence, isolation, depression, anxiety, and fear become part of their everyday experience. A strong and aware mental health support is essential to help them navigate through these difficult emotions. Queer and trans affirmative sports psychologists can be a solid support for this vulnerable group of athletes.** | |
| **Educate self** | Read about trans realities<br>Understand their contexts and struggles to address their distress better<br>Update yourself on evolving laws and policies related to trans rights |
| **Check own biases** | You are a part of this heavily biased and unjust world<br>It is important to check your own biases and beliefs about trans persons in general and trans athletes in particular<br>Read more and understand trans issues to better help in guiding policy making |

By following these practices, we can cultivate a sports culture that not only welcomes but actively supports and celebrates athletes of all genders. When inclusivity becomes a fundamental principle in sports, it fosters an environment where everyone, regardless of gender, feels valued, respected, and empowered to participate and excel.

A more inclusive and equitable approach to sports not only benefits athletes but also sets a powerful example for society as a whole. When we prioritize fairness and diversity in athletics, we send a strong message that differences should be embraced rather than excluded. This commitment to inclusion can have a ripple effect, inspiring change beyond the playing field by encouraging workplaces, schools, and communities to adopt similar values of respect and acceptance.

Ultimately, making sports more inclusive is not just about fairness—it's about creating a space where every individual has the opportunity to thrive. When we work together to break down barriers and challenge outdated norms, we build a more united and understanding society—one where diversity is not only acknowledged but celebrated in every arena of life.

# SPORT PERFORMANCE & UNCONSCIOUS PROCESSES -

PRIYANKA PRABHAKAR &
DR. CHAITANYA SRIDHAR

Sport is more than just a game! Winning shots, supreme confidence and resilience make sports exciting for any of us to watch. However, have you ever wondered what made a cricketer rise to the occasion and score the winning century? What made the best striker miss a penalty shot in a decisive game? What processes did the celebrated swimmer use to overcome the mental block of performing on home ground? How did the female athletes reach an empowered state and play skillfully in a culture where their abilities were doubted? How did a young prodigy overcome his fears and start playing to his full potential in the competition?

What do you think the above questions are about? Let's take some time and reflect on them. First of all, the questions reflect on the mental processes that the athletes have adapted for their performance. It makes us wonder what mental processes helped an athlete to score the winning century, and simultaneously, what happened in the mind of the best striker to miss the opportunity. It brings to light that if mental processes are followed with discipline, it could give us the desired results.

If you analyse deeper, these questions could also give us insights into the conscious and unconscious aspects of the performance of athletes and sports teams. In the classical psychoanalytic theory of Sigmund Freud, the region of the psyche that contains thoughts, feelings, perceptions, and other aspects of mental life currently present in awareness formed the conscious aspects.

The region of the psyche containing memories, emotional conflicts, wishes, and repressed impulses that are not directly accessible to awareness but that have dynamic effects on thought and behaviour is formed by the unconscious (APA Dictionary of Psychology). In simple words, the conscious aspects consist of the feelings, memories, and wishes a person is aware of, and the unconscious aspects consist of all the thoughts, beliefs, and feelings which a person is not aware of.

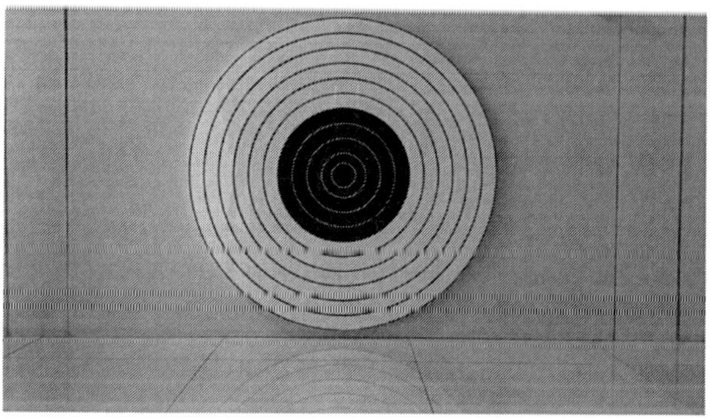

**Picture Courtesy - Dharthi Chipalkatti**

As we are talking about conscious and unconscious processes of performance, we want to bring to your notice that sports psychologists use many psychological techniques that help understand the conscious and unconscious aspects of an athlete's performance.

Sometimes, sports psychologists use certain techniques to work with athletes based on the thoughts, feelings that the athlete is already aware of or conscious of, such as goal setting, visualization, mental plans for competition, etc. Psychologists also use specific techniques to help athletes become aware of the thoughts and beliefs which are hidden from their conscious awareness i.e, unconscious processes. Projective techniques, hypnotherapy, somatic therapy and creative movement therapy, dream analysis, and systemic family constellation are some of the methods that help bring the unconscious thoughts and patterns to awareness.

In our experience as practitioners, the psychological techniques that bring awareness to the unconscious thoughts, feelings that are hidden from conscious awareness, i.e., the unconscious techniques, help us get a deeper understanding of the core issues faced by athletes. The hidden thoughts and dynamics of athletes could be revealed to us through narrative, phrases, images, dreams, family history, body language, etc. There is a reason some of the thoughts and feelings are unconscious and hidden; that is because it could contain hidden family loyalties, painful experiences of childhood, the shadow self, taboos, etc. When a person integrates all of this, he becomes a whole person, which further empowers him towards performance.

Let's look at an example where a psychologist integrates the unconscious aspects in the sports field. A young boxer was dissociated during the bout, which led her to lose from a winning position against an elite boxer. Suddenly becoming the crowd favourite, it was against what she expected, and unknowingly, she lost her centre and consequently disassociated. With the psychologist's help, the young boxer understood her inner narrative of 'not being good enough' since she was in the shadows of an elite boxer.

Gradually, she began claiming her own power. Then, she was able to take charge of the upcoming competitions and eventually won the matches.

**How does this area of work help our athletes?**

As sports psychology practitioners, we have most often noticed that athletes/coaches/parents reach out to us to work on the following issues: competitive anxiety, building confidence, managing self, coach, and parental expectations, work-life balance, injury management, team building, and enhancing coach-athlete-team relationships.

We will give you some examples of how we use psychotherapeutic techniques to help our athletes with their unconscious. Firstly, as practitioners, we are compassionate about the psychological issues that are unique to each athlete. Secondly, we are curious to understand the root cause of the behaviour; we use appropriate psychotherapeutic techniques to bring to light the thoughts, feelings, and fears which are hidden from the athletes' conscious awareness.

Let us look at some case examples where the athletes have become aware of their hidden thoughts, feelings, and coping mechanisms.

A long-distance runner was frequently injured, and the medical team suspected psychological issues as one of the causes of injury. Through psychology sessions, deeper analysis of the athlete revealed how she was over-relying on the medical team for emotional support; frequent injuries have helped her deal with loneliness and lack of family support she experienced as a child.

When the problem is brought into the conscious awareness of the athlete, she could develop healthier ways of coping with loneliness and seeking emotional support.

A 100 m sprinter has recurrent dreams of falling from a high-rise building two weeks prior to an important competitive event. By working on the dreams of the athlete, the psychologist brought to light self-doubts, anxiety, and fear of failure. The athlete approached the concern with insight and began working on his fears.

A footballer learned that his struggles with perfectionism, high expectations, and battling anxiety were related to the trauma of losing his sibling way early in life. The focus was on acknowledging his grief and loss of losing his sibling and moving towards embracing his life and sports with passion.

A basketball player found it difficult to build relationships with teammates and play as a team because she was always expected to fulfil the desires of her father's unfulfilled sports dream. Her core belief was that if she played as a team, it meant she wouldn't get the attention that she longed for from her father. Understanding this unconscious pattern helped the athlete to make the right choices for her team and sports.

From the above examples, we can see that as practitioners, we look at athletes' experiences holistically. An understanding of the family, culture, dreams, coping patterns, and trauma helps us empower athletes and develop compassion in their lives and training. Dwelling deep into some of these techniques helped athletes to be kinder to themselves and to their life experiences, and gave them insights which helped them find answers to the issues that engulfed them.

As sport psychologists, our personal journeys of understanding our own thoughts, feelings, which were hidden from our conscious awareness, also make us advocate these techniques. A famous quote which guides us is by Dr Carl Jung: "Until you make the unconscious conscious, it will direct your life and you will call it fate".

Keeping these insights in mind, we bring in our training from Jungian depth psychology and systemic family constellation in this chapter.

## Dream Analysis and Systemic Family Constellation

Albeit, there are multiple approaches such as Cognitive Behavioral Therapy (CBT), Acceptance and Commitment Therapy, Emotion Focused Therapy etc., which sport psychologists use to work with athletes. All the approaches mentioned above help athletes to achieve their peak performance. In this chapter, we primarily integrate Jungian depth psychology and Systemic Family Constellation to aid the players in achieving peak performance. Let us understand more about dream analysis and Systemic Family Constellation.

## Dream analysis

Dreams are the powerhouse of the psyche and can provide timely insights to support athletes. Dr. Carl Jung developed analytical psychology, which brought the soul to an overly rational approach His theory and lifetime work emphasised working with the unconscious and allowing the psyche to guide therapy.

Importantly, Jung was the pioneer in integrating dreams into work with an individual without reducing them down!

Let's take an example of dream analysis in sports psychology. An athlete at the world stage had repeated dreams of being taken over on the podium.

Whilst the psychologist understood the meaning, the athlete was prodded to reflect, and gradually he realized that it was an inner figure guiding him to push himself a little more. The minute he had the 'aha' moment, he made the intention to get over his laid-back attitude which had been a primary concern. This was a pivotal dream that guided him to enhance performance during his career. Whilst dreams may seem nonsensical to many, they have deep meaning that needs to be worked through by a trained professional. Animal figures in dreams and their relation to the dreamer can also provide insights and support to the individual.

## Systemic Family Constellation

Systemic Family Constellation was developed by German Psychoanalyst Bert Hellinger. In the field of sports, this therapeutic approach could bring to light the family patterns of an athlete, which keeps a person stuck in the past and make way for new thoughts and beliefs that aid sports performance. For example, let's consider a basketball player who did not get selected to the state team and was overtraining to get selected in the upcoming event. The athlete believed he would not be strong if he acknowledged his emotions of shame, anger, and sadness. The psychologist explored what made the athlete strong/weak. By understanding his family better, the athlete realized a few things about his father. His father was the firstborn; he had a lot of responsibilities since he lost his father early in life. His father chose to keep working as a form of coping instead of exploring and being compassionate to himself. The athlete had learned the same from his father and was overworking to cope with his emotions and life. The athlete learned that being gentle with himself is also a sign of strength. Here, the psychologist, by working with the athlete over time, brings to light the unconscious family patterns that influenced his coping.

Balance, order, and belonging are the three guiding principles of Family Constellation.

## Integrating dream analysis and family constellation

As mentioned previously, there is so much that athletes could learn about themselves through their unconscious and hidden thoughts, fears, and desires. In this section, we try to bring in our work experiences using dream analysis and family constellation, and integrate the approaches.

## Case study 1

An athlete had a repetitive dream that he was almost reaching the finish line, but someone overtakes him at the last minute and he loses the race. He comes second in the dream. The psychologist knew the athlete well and had worked with him for quite a while. As the sessions progressed, the athlete became aware that the one who was overtaking him was not a known competitor, but it was his own inner self which was encouraging him to move forward as he had more potential than what he was utilising. The dream brought up an interesting aspect of awareness for the athlete- it made him reflect that he needs to transform his lazy attitude and perform to his potential. The session implemented dream analysis, which helped the athlete to work and channel energy for an important competitive event. This dream had also repeated and was crucial in the athlete's journey to propel forward.

## Alternative case:

A young cricketer often doubted his potential and would overthink that was detrimental to his performance. Before a major tournament, he dreams of working out in the gym with a senior he admires. Post the session, his trainer applauds his workout and says, "he has more energy than the senior". The dream integration helped him understand that he was belittling himself and ought to believe in his ability and hard work. Here the trainer was a supportive inner-figure that supported the athlete personally, too as the core belief was that 'he was not good enough'. Hence, he would overtrain which led to injury at crucial competitions. As he got a better understanding of his inner workings, he began approaching challenges with adventure. This leads to embracing responsibility and competition with joy, rather than just out of fear.

## Case study 2

A 30-year-old tennis player dreams of war and destruction around him before a major competitive event. He dreamt that he was sitting in a telephone booth and is with a stranger who was supporting him to talk about what happened and seek help. But the athlete isn't able to express himself. He just gives up. He sees people fighting all around him, blames himself, and is filled with grief. The athlete was going through a transformation in his personal life when he had this dream. The dream brought to awareness the violence he had witnessed as a child. The athlete became conscious of how he had difficulty expressing and seeking help because of his early childhood trauma. He recognised that under extreme stress, he had a coping pattern of blaming himself, as this was his way of gaining control and power over the situation.

The psychologist worked on healthy ways of coping, expressing himself, and developing self-compassion. The other person in the telephone booth was an inner supportive figure supporting the athlete in this juncture. We can greatly aid athletes through the guidance from the individual's psyche.

The strength of dream analysis and systemic family constellation techniques lies in empowering the individuals to lead life with understanding, wisdom, and making them a whole person. These techniques bring union to the fragmented parts of the self, reduce anxiety, and enhance coping mechanisms in the individual. It also helps in enabling interpersonal relationships and leads life with authenticity. It can then aid in emotional regulation and decision making, thereby helping with performance Challenges to using techniques that specialize in making the unconscious conscious

**There are challenges in making an athlete aware of unconscious thoughts and patterns.**

1. Sports psychology is important in sports; however, in the Indian context, we still have a long way to go to build awareness on the importance of taking care of the thoughts, feelings, and emotions and how it impacts sports performance.
2. The stakeholders of the sporting system need to be integrated; majority of the time, athletes are able to access the services of psychologists through the organisations, federations, or parents. It is important to create awareness among these key stakeholders.
3. It is important for psychologists to train in other holistic therapy techniques which could help them to be more present and authentic to athletes and their concerns competently. These techniques could be developed by psychologists through certifications and courses from recognized universities and institutions. However, the courses being expensive and the training protocols being extensive could be a challenge.
4. Psychologists ought to invest time in their own self-work, so that their issues are not projected onto the athlete/team. This helps in

enabling and empowering the athletes. Hence, self-work needs to be a priority for psychologists.

5. Athletes may not be regular with their psychology sessions; there are chances they may drop out after one session, which affects the progress of work.

## Cultural considerations

From our experience, the psychotherapeutic techniques help uncover hidden thoughts and feelings; aware/ conscious can be used very well with the Indian population.

1. Indian athletes seem to be receptive to understanding their strengths, resilience, and grit, knowing their traumas, cultural conditioning, and family patterns. There is an openness to learn more than what they already know, and there is also an eagerness to be conscious of those aspects which they have no idea about.
2. Athletes understand that their body, other than helping them with performance and being strong, stores insights and wisdom. This brings in a new way to look at the body.
3. The techniques help athletes to understand their thought patterns and change them positively. Athletes are no longer stuck in their patterns of the past. It is in-depth work which may initially cause distress and eventually lead to healing.

## Reflections

### For athletes and parents

1. There is stigma around seeking help from a professional psychologist. The role of the mind and body is equally important in the field of sports to reach peak performance. Don't hesitate to contact a professional psychologist to work on well-being and performance.
2. It is important to be regular for the mental training sessions. It takes some time to develop the necessary mental skills, and it is important to be patient with expectations.

### For practitioners

1. As a psychologist, it is important to use intuition and wisdom as well in the work.
2. Being trained with the correct techniques and institutions is necessary while learning about techniques to work with the unconscious. When the techniques are learned without an adequate theoretical framework and guidance, it could cause more harm to the athletes than do good.
3. Regular supervision with qualified professionals will help sport psychologists understand if they are getting entangled with the athletes' problems.
4. Seeking help to work on our professional boundaries will help us work for the highest good of the athletes.

# THE NEED FOR SUPERVISED PRACTICE IN INDIAN SPORT PSYCHOLOGY: PRESENT CHALLENGES AND WAY AHEAD -

VARADAYINI GORHE &
KEERTHANA SWAMINATHAN

Before we start holding a higher ground by speaking from a pedestal, let us understand the definition of supervision in psychology. Supervision is a formal understanding and agreement between a training psychologist and an experienced psychologist. This understanding helps the trainee discuss their applied practice with a skilled psychologist. This also ensures that the young psychologist is supported in their professional development journey.

Now that we have established supervision's primary aim, we must consider its need in a country like India, especially for sports psychology. Formal supervision hasn't found its ground in any field of psychology apart from clinical psychology. In any master-level programme of sport psychology, the student is exposed to research and practical experience on a surface level. Unless you do a specialised course, for example, REBT Advanced certification through the Ellis Institute, you do not get supervised training.

**Why is Supervision necessary for sports psychologists in India?**

Sport Psychology practice is a relatively young field in India, with only a small pool of trained professionals—those who have completed a master's or PhD in sport psychology. While having a master's in psychology with a specialisation in sports is deemed mandatory, the amount of practice exposure given to someone who has an MSc from the U.K. or someone who has a brief unsupervised exposure to client interactions through a Master's in Sport Psychology in India is very short. Hence, early-career sport psychologists or neophytes need to be guided through their first two years to ensure that they stick to certain mandated or standardised protocols. The following are the common reasons why supervision should be made mandatory.

## Ethical Codes Compliance

Supervision helps ensure that neophyte sport psychologists practice within the ethical guidelines, thus protecting the well-being of their clients and their profession. While supervised, neophytes can also bounce off their ethical dilemmas without contemplating new situations. For instance, recently, a trainee sports psychologist asked whether she could take up sessions for twins who worked in her academy. While there was no alternative present (as she is the only sport psychologist), she started her work with words of caution about not exchanging any notes from one sibling to the other.

## Skill Development

Supervision provides a platform for ongoing learning and skill development, helping neophyte psychologists stay up-to-date with their field's latest techniques and research. Supervisors offer constructive feedback on the sport psychologist's performance, identifying areas for improvement and providing guidance on enhancing their practice. Secondly, supervisors also help develop a scientist-practitioner mindset that makes a sport psychologist curious about learning and developing research skills. For instance, trainees can be provided with reading material for the month. This ensures that they are given some thought-provoking insights into the field and there is a fair exchange of thoughts on the same once it is sent.

## Case Consultation

Supervisors can provide support and guidance when dealing with complex or challenging cases, helping sport psychologists develop effective intervention strategies. This also means guiding them on whether to address specific areas of problems and competence that go beyond their area of expertise.

Recently, a trainee spoke to one of us about how her client opened up about sustained emotional abuse from her home, and she needed to seek some more help that included family counselling. While a supervisor should allow their trainee to express interaction with their client and reflections, the trainee thought that she would need to stop her sessions until she resolved the trauma. However, we advised her to continue offering parallel sport psychology sessions as her goal with the client would differ from the family counsellor. In such cases, guidance from an experienced professional can help foster a healthier Sport Psychologist-Client relationship.

## Professional Accountability

Supervision helps ensure that sports psychologists provide high-quality services to their clients. Supervisors can hold psychologists accountable for their actions and help them develop a sense of professional responsibility.

This also means that a neophyte is highly responsible for protecting the profession of sport psychology and the client's welfare. A simple example of not referring a client to a specialist because one may lose financial gains means the Sport Psychologist is bringing down the trust, thereby creating a space of doubt in the client's mind for the whole community of sport psychologists.

## The present set of Challenges in India

Even though many of us may acknowledge the above benefits of supervision, there are specific barriers and challenges that a neophyte sports psychologist will face while looking to get supervised in India, after a Master's degree in Sport Psychology.

## Lack of standardised education programmes

Whether one studies at an international university or from an Indian university, there is no standardisation in the modules that are studied and applied in India. For example, some Indian universities focus on sports science in the first year, whereas many other universities offer counselling to be a primary module in their programme. Unfortunately, this does not help in promoting a competence based approach that helps choose the right supervisors.

For example, a student who is about to graduate with an MSc in Sport Psychology from a university has a keen inclination on working with corporates or sports organisations. But his education did not cover much of organisational behaviour or psychology. This also does not let him choose a supervisor who has an in-depth understanding of the niche as he has no module exposure to the core competence.

## There is no compulsion for supervision in India to practice

Unlike many other countries, where a licensing process or accreditation is compulsory before private or independent practice, India does not account for any legal ramifications of not obtaining licensure for a practising psychologist. The most crucial aspect of licensure or accreditation is supervised practice.

However, due to the absence of such legal requirements, supervision is often overlooked.

## The know-it-all Attitude

One can say, fame supersedes knowledge in India. Most sport psychology graduates feel they know everything about sport psychology and it is only they who can make a significant impact on the athlete's career. With this attitude, many fail to pursue the importance of working under someone senior. Many may also not believe in spending money to seek guidance from a senior.

This same attitude is prevalent when psychologists need to seek therapy for their benefit.

## Although minor, these factors are a critical mirror of the nearly

non-existent supervision culture in the field of sport psychology in India. So now, how do we senior sport psychologists find a middle ground or a way ahead?

## Next steps for developing a culture of supervised practice in India

1. ***Include 50% supervised practice in a master's course***. If a university has a 2-year degree, a part of your degree includes on-field experience under a senior sport psychologist. This supervised practice should be logged and reported. Written assessments and Vivas should be conducted to help the neophyte develop confidence over the hours of supervised practice.
2. ***Mentoring and supervision under a senior sport psychologist.*** Any sport psychologist graduated from India or any other country should have compulsory supervised practice under a reputed and qualified sport psychologist, preferably a sport psychologist who is training or trained to become a supervisor. These supervised hours should be in line with an international association like the ISSP, BASES or AASP.
3. ***Hiring processes at sports organisations***. Any High Performing Centre or team who is hiring a sport psychologist with limited experience should also hire a supervising sport psychologist to monitor the programme. This is especially valid if the hired sports psychologist does not have a supervisor.
4. National Centres of Excellence (NCoEs) and National Governing Bodies (NGBs) should hire sports psychologists with at least 1 year of experience or supervision under a senior qualified sport psychologist. Hiring freshers with less or no experience may be easy financially, but won't help in generating the right practice with the athletes.
5. Educational institutes and sports organisations should collaborate with larger associations like ISSP (International Society of Sport Psychology), INSPA (INSPA Association of Sport Psychologists), SPAI, BASES (British Association of Sport and Exercise Sciences), or AASP (Association of Applied Sport Psychology). This will ensure that educational institutes partner with the

correct supervisors who are qualified by the associations. It will also help sports bodies, NCOEs, and NGBs to hire the correct sport psychologist who has been a registered member or who is supervised by the association-recognised supervisor. Individuals could also consider getting registered through ISSP (ISSP-R). If this becomes a part of the organisation's hiring requirements, it will help standardise the profession.

To conclude, the most important thing to understand is that the motto of supervision isn't to say one's methods are good or bad. It only exists so that the practitioners can work through challenging periods and situations in the best possible manner. Mistakes are inevitable, but the fact that one needs to have the mindset to factor that in and acknowledge it makes a significant difference. The key to us becoming the best version of ourselves is continued education, development, and supervision.

**Reflection Questions:**

Before approaching a supervisor, do ask yourself the following questions:

1. As a recently graduated master's in sport psychology, what are the areas of competence I need to develop to have a better on-ground understanding of practicing sport psychology?
2. What school of psychology do I adhere to the most and why?
3. What areas of psychology- performance and mental health, do I need more training in? Why?
4. Does my prospective supervisor hold significant experience and a steady professional philosophy in sport psychology?
5. Does my prospective supervisor hold additional qualifications to undertake supervision?

# FIELD OF POTENTIAL: THE EMERGING FLOW STATE -

DR. CHAITANYA SRIDHAR

*"There is a perfect shot waiting for you, all you need to do is get yourself out of the way"*

**– Caddy to a champion golfer**

The intention of this chapter is to provide the essence of my work and how I came to develop the 'Field of Potential' (FOP) to aid the emergence of athletes' flow state.

The quote above succinctly explains the concept to empower athletes to reach their peak potential.

Let's start from the beginning of my journey. In fact, I had to be pushed by my professor to attend the sports psychology interview at the Sports Authority of India (SAI). I vividly recall telling her that I really didn't know much about the field.

She seemed to have more confidence in me and reassured me, saying that it's basically applying the principles of psychology to sport and performance. Obviously, I couldn't let my professor down, so I prepared a little, and surprisingly, I thoroughly enjoyed the interview. And as they say, "the rest is history".

Quite early in my career, I got recognised by the Sports Ministry for my work with an athlete who broke the Asian Games record. I was quite young and was practically just beginning my journey. If you look at where I was then and where I am now, I still continue in the same way, though I think the two-word 'Dr' title and having gone abroad are probably looked at differently but in essence, I still function the same.

In fact, I usually say that both sports psychology and the elephants chose me and not the other way around. So, I embraced my fate and made it my destiny, and it truly has been an adventure with all its ups and downs.

Then, moving forward, I went to Australia for my PhD. During this time, I attended and presented at the ISSP conference. This was a pivotal point in my career as I met one of my mentors, and his approach continues to inspire me. Dr. Kenneth Raveza's working philosophy is very much in line with my views, though we sadly lost him during COVID.

I'd like you to imagine a young, introverted, and perhaps the only Indian or even Asian attending the pre-conference workshop. Since he couldn't pronounce my name, he said, "Oh, I'm going to call you Ms. Bangalore", though I protested, it kind of broke the ice. Needless to say, I thoroughly enjoyed the workshop. In hindsight, that experience helped set the tone for my presentation, especially after a not-so-good one at the University. I took on the pressure of being the first Indian in the department, resulting in a mediocre presentation. Talk of performance and pressure!

So, I was presenting at the Symposium on mental toughness the next day and wanted to get a feel of the place. As I was waiting for the proceedings to end, he came up and enquired about my presentation. I nodded, and I sure understood my state as I pictured myself in the huge Tumbalong auditorium and wondered why it wasn't in one of the smaller halls.

He patiently waited till the crowd abated, gently held my hand, and led me up the steps of the stage. Then he pointed to the far end of the green exit sign. I'll never forget when he advised me to breathe every time I saw it. No prizes for guessing it was the first thing that I did and till date perhaps one of my best presentations. I really was flowing, and what Dr. Raveza did was help me to my best possible state.

---

> *"Safety is not just the mere absence of threat, safety is the presence of connection"*
>
> **– Dr. Porges**

---

The more I reflect on this, what he really did was being truly present to another, just a budding sports psych whom he could have overseen, but he made that effort, an authentic connection, and reassured, "you're going to do great". How often we underestimate the power of belief, the power of a holding presence. Post the symposium, he immediately came up and told me that I did great. It's like getting a special session with your mentor.

> Thought Box: Reflecting on your journey
>
> Let's take a moment to pause and reflect upon your journey.
>
> - Who supported, uplifted, or guided you during an important juncture? (Be it a match or performance, was it a mentor, coach, or peer?)
> - How did you feel before, during, and after the connection?
> - What transpired as a result of that experience?

Hold this experience close to you and build on it as you move forward with your career. Perhaps now, you are in a position to influence another.

In fact, with athletes, I usually ask them about their best performance and build it to their FOP. The shift in energy is palpable, leading the way to their zone/best state to compete.

**Continuing my journey in India**

Moving forward, I came back to India. I began noticing that even after a single session, athletes would go on to win a medal. When credited, I would always, always, say, "No, it's not me but the athlete". Over time, I realised that it's the 'space/ field' akin to a hockey field or the cricket ground. Here, it's the psychological space. Even when it's an online session with the athlete or team, it's about me being fully present.

First, I must be present with myself; only then can I be present for the athlete. When I've taken the time to tune into the space, at times, I can predict or perceive what's going to come up, because I'm aligned energetically as well. It's vital to be able to tune into the space, be it psychological or energetic, whatever one chooses to call it. True connection and magic happen there!

> Be like water making its way through cracks. Do not be assertive, but adjust to the object, and you shall find a way around or through it. If nothing within you stays rigid, outward things will disclose themselves.
>
> Empty your mind, be formless. Shapeless, like water. If you put water into a cup, it becomes the cup. You put water into a bottle and it becomes the bottle. You put it in a teapot, it becomes the teapot. Now, water can flow or it can crash. Be water, my friend.
>
> Bruce Lee

Now, I want to bring in the case of a young swimmer with whom I had been working for a while. He'd won the state championship, and it was the session just before the nationals. During the goal setting, I noticed there was hardly any difference between the current and target time. The dialogue was as follows:

CS- What's happening here?

SW- Oh, but if I go below this time, I'm going to be beating X's record (who was one of India's top swimmers at that point in time).

I paused for a minute and thankfully didn't say, "Oh, come on, you can beat him", as that would have only raised his defences. He might still have been polite and nodded, but deep down, at the subconscious level, he didn't believe it was possible. Because this elite athlete, whom I'm going to call Rajiv, was larger than life. Our young swimmer has seen him as a young kid and perhaps projected the qualities of a hero, right? Before reading ahead, take a moment to think about what can be said or done in such situations. The clue lies in Bruce Lee's quote on water.

This is how I approached the case.

"Okay, you know where you are right now, keeping in mind your coach's feedback and your training. Have a look at the timing once again and let's see what happens".

If you notice, rather than directly saying, 'you can break the record', I was more subtle. I also added, "Oh, you know, before Rajiv's record, it was someone else's and then another person's record too". No surprises, he went on to break two records out of three because he focused on his potential at the meet and not how great Rajiv is. He was able to 'Be like water and FLOW'.

More recently, a similar incident occurred with another young swimmer who was going through quite a few challenges. As we were working through it, I remembered 'it's about giving yourself the chance', that's what the caddy is saying, 'your best chance on that possible day, because you really don't know what is possible; you also don't know where the other athletes stand', right? She went on to win the gold and broke the national record, which had been held for 13 years by one of India's best swimmers. So, what's actually happening here? You begin to look into what the individual/athlete's needs are at any given point in time. Also, am I really connecting at a deep level, or am I just being superficial? This understanding came to me when the elephants entered my life, which was also the beginning point of my Jungian depth psychology training, it's about being attuned to the other and to the field to influence positively.

This is the same principle I apply to elephants.

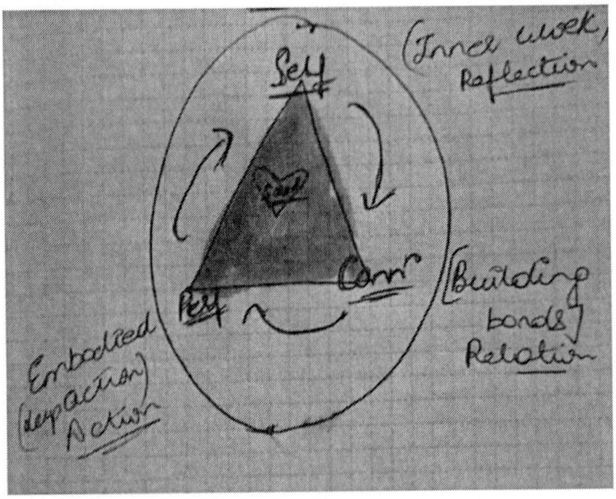


For example, Leela is a young elephant (also writing about this in my elephant book). The minute we met for the first time, I asked, "Are you Leela?" She gave a low rumble, started vocalizing, and soon she offered me her trunk as a way to connect. Obviously, her mahout (caretaker) was as surprised and shocked as me. It's really your presence, your personality, and who you are at the deepest level that influences how you relate to others and how you come about, so self-work is very important, especially being a psychologist.

---

> *"The meeting of two personalities is like the contact of two chemical substances. If there is any reaction, both are transformed"*
>
> **– Carl Jung**

---

Imagine, if I'm talking just from the head, overly rational, I'm going to be disembodied, then how can I support the athlete, right? We see this a lot with sports personnel.

Let's look at this athlete who was a youth Olympian when we first met. Now, a leading athlete and an Olympian. On one occasion, I was getting urgent session requests from the coach. The athlete was highly stressed but kept repeating "I'm fine, ma'am". It took a while, but gradually I mirrored the calm state needed for a dialogue and brought him to a reasonably open mindset where he had a chance to perform, despite his technique having been changed recently. He went on to win as he stopped catastrophising the outcome. This process of building trust at such crucial times aided his Olympic journey too. He would often want to talk to me before competitions. What he was seeking was a connection, knowing him helped in working through various challenges in the journey.

Gradually, we also realized that he would get a little ahead of himself. So, what needed to be done was to bring him back to the body. We figured a stance as well, which worked for him, so his mind wasn't racing a thousand miles per hour. Building an embodied ritual to help him stay grounded to perform and be himself was crucial.

At this juncture, I'd like to bring in the case of a young golfer, which impacted me quite a bit. The teen golfer had an issue with standing out and would lose from a winning position. It's essential to work through and understand what was happening with her, right? Rather than jumping to conclusions. The coach made a key point that she came from a single-parent family (he said "broken family"). Initially, the pressure of not disappointing the struggling single parent was what came up. Also, I realised she had an extremely introverted personality. When we went into the details on what attention meant for her, the memory of being beaten came up. This had to be handled and treated very gently since she was quite young. Gradually, as the athlete felt safe with me, she began to trust that she could integrate this wounded inner child of hers.

Consequently, she started winning and enjoying the right attention. It was moving to see her embrace her inner child, and she would often say, "I would remember what you said (psychologist) and hold myself, Ma'am".

To this day, this is one of the most cherished memories of enabling an athlete, as I knew we had worked through and integrated a core issue, else it would have been a debilitating concern in her future life.

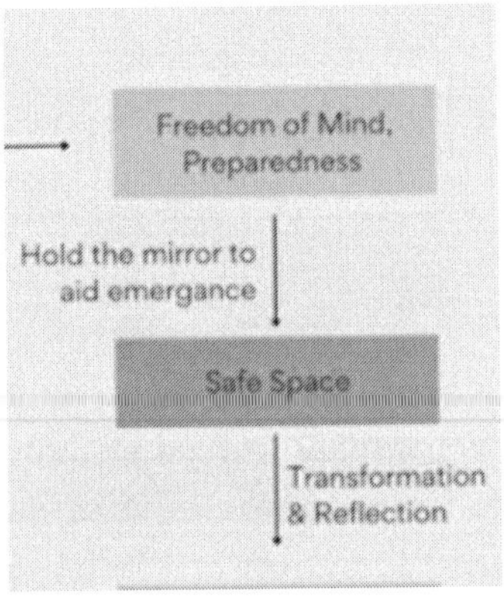


Now, I'd like to invite you to ponder what comes up for you as you read this case example. How would you have dealt with this athlete and such scenarios? Remember, there is no one way.

Right from the beginning of my sport psychology career, I felt the overemphasis on performance alone was lopsided, as it failed to take the whole individual into consideration. I sought and gradually integrated holistic healing modalities and then depth psychology principles to enable and empower the whole individual.

One of the first things I noticed was the importance of the athlete's narrative— the deeper story behind their journey. Athletes might not be aware of their core beliefs, especially at a deeper, unconscious level. Understanding this narrative is crucial, as it allows us to explore intrinsic motivation and potential blocks.

To this day, I have former players tell me I changed their lives just by believing in them.

The biggest gift I've received from the elephants has been authentic connections. We are all part of one field and influencing each other, and that's where the magic happens.

It's essential to embody ourselves first (not just in the head) to better equip those we work with. The archetype of the healer and mentoring is in the 'psychological space', and how much self-work I have done will also greatly impact my ability to support athlete transformation, in addition to performance. I remember Olympic medallist Sakshi Mallik saying it is truly gratifying when youngsters, especially from remote regions, would credit her for playing sports. We know she's moved from being successful to inspirational.

Early on, I called the FOP (Field of Potential) "Emergence".

Whilst working with one of the super elite teams, I was explaining the process of emergence, similar to the potential that we're delving into. The intention is to curiously explore what can emerge when we're in a prepared and open state. Incidentally, I was at the centre of the circle, and on the screen was my photo with two of our lovely elephants. As I explained the emergence phenomenon, something opened and emerged. I could see the awe in their eyes as I elucidated it through my connection to elephants. It was almost like, "Okay, if she can handle elephants, she can handle anything (and us)".

In fact, before the session, I checked with the head coach if I could connect it to the elephants, and was expecting a vehement negative, but he just jumped at the idea. So, that's how I've begun integrating my two worlds, because animals are instinctual and have much to teach us, too. As much as sport is instinctual, it is very often forgotten and ignored.

When an athlete is performing, or when they're in a flow state, they're embodied- mind and body together. On the contrary, when you see an athlete during and after a below-par tournament or under severe pressure, you'll invariably see that they're dissociated and disconnected from their body, from themselves, and others.

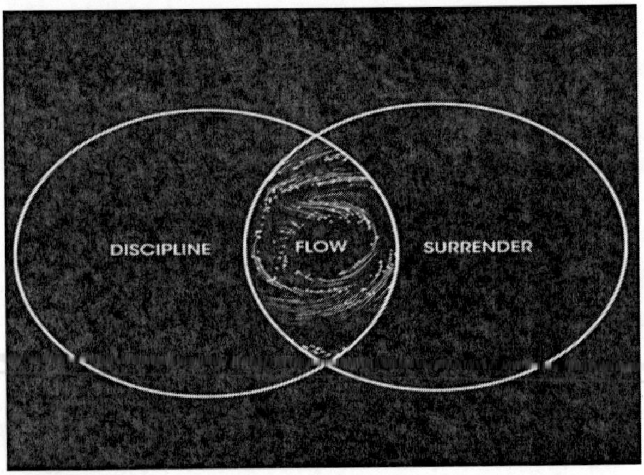


**Alan Watts on Flow**

As I've reflected more on my journey, I've strived to first build authentic connections before embarking on anything else. Also, there is no one solution that fits all athletes. For example, an elite boxer will inform me of the time of her bout, and all I need to say is "Go for it, champ", another may want a session and see me. Essentially, to understand what clicks for each athlete.

So, to understand what the need is, where the problem is, and what is it that can be done? In my experience, this is crucial, along with helping athletes to prepare and embody peak performance. In fact, I was influenced, at least earlier in my career, by Yuri Hanin's Individual Zone of Optimal Functioning (IZOF) and gradually realized the flow state by Dr. Mihaly is quite similar, but I still felt there was something missing for my work. Now, I mainly work with the FOP, and must admit I've grown in the process too.

In fact, I understood and integrated the embodied approach in my Jungian Training, mainly via Embodied Imagination and Body Dreaming as we bring focus to the felt sense whilst working with an image, be it of a dream or otherwise.

---

> *"Know all the theories, master all the techniques. But as you touch a human soul, be just another human soul"*
>
> **– Carl Jung!**

---

When I'm asked if I counsel or motivate athletes being a sport psychologist, my response is that I hold the mirror to their emergence, highest potential.

The world witnessed the youngest chess champion, Gukesh, who channelled his emotions and made history!

Honestly, this is what I aim to do: hold the athlete, understand them, look at the core of what the concern is, and then work on the intervention. Also, many times you hold hope amidst true despair, until the athlete can bounce back and re-emerge.

Let me elucidate using the example of an Olympian I once worked with. When I first met her, she was going through immense challenges. However, as we worked through, a glimmer of hope emerged.

"The minute I see you, I feel everything's fine" is what she'd say as she was working through the tough process. If I had tried to rush the process or focused on sport alone, we would have perhaps lost her from Indian Sport.

Another athlete who competed at the Paris Olympics recently was seeing me post Olympics. He had an injury and other things going on, but displayed a resilient spirit.

When he recognised me at the far end of the cafeteria, he came running and gave me a big, tight hug and said, “Finally”. Finally, meaning you’re here.

This is the work, creating a safe space for the person to rebuild themselves. Just being there and seeing them through everything. Admirers are plenty when things are going well, but it’s even more essential to support them during lows, the challenges.

2024 has been a comeback year for me as I re-emerged through a major surgery, and I know how important it is to have support. In a country that idolises success and demonises when expectations are not met, it’s vital to be a constant pillar of support.

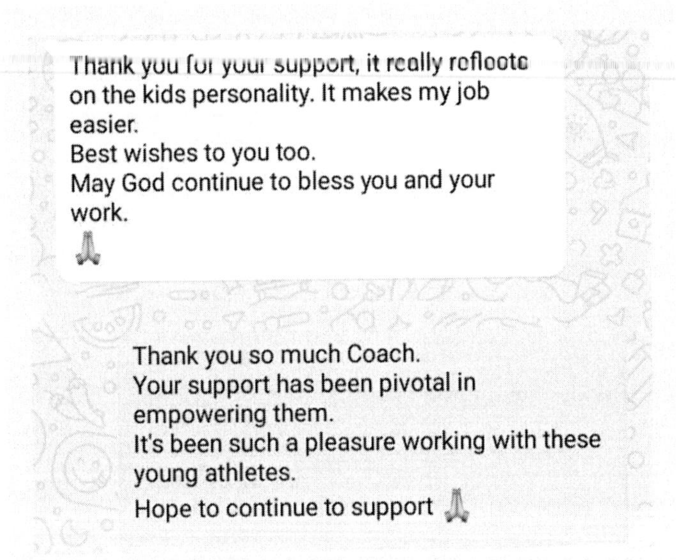


Even now, I have people saying you changed my life, and I feel like that’s what we want to do, because the shelf life is relatively less in sport. At an event, Abhinav Bindra apparently said, “I wish I were more human” about his sporting journey. No wonder he is such a huge proponent of mental health in sport now.

"My greatest triumphs and my most catastrophic failures have been a direct result of the state of my mind. Being in a positive emotional state simply helps one feel physically lighter, stay more present in the moment and make better decisions.

I remember a summer when I was undergoing significant emotional turmoil. I was extremely vulnerable and miserable. One day when the speed gun was brought to measure our bowling speeds, I tensed up and overthought my way to the ridiculous conclusion that this day would somehow make or break my career. I made myself so physically stiff and unstable that I bowled only at 97kmph. The nerves made a pit in my stomach, my legs felt heavy and I simply couldn't manage to get myself into my normal bowling rhythm.

I obsessed about this failure for the next 2 days and made a mess of the match. I felt like my career and my life was slipping away. I asked for a session and discussed this with Dr Sridhar. I remember the first words when i said maybe i should quit were " Come on, you are much stronger than this". Then, she went on to remind me of how i had worked my way to every sporting achievement.

In an instant from that perspective the fact that i had a few bad weeks felt miniscule in comparison to what i had already manged to get through. When she held out a mirror, i actually found my most insurmountable problems to be quite surmountable. This was where she had a very significant impact on me.
She made me to be mindful and ask myself 'is this relevant now?' whenever i had a limiting thought.

A couple of days after the session, I had a practice game and had to put in a good performance. I was still slightly nervous but manged to stay calm enough. I ended up with 4 wickets for 17 runs in 6 overs.
It changed everything in an instant. I went from being very quiet, avoiding eye contact and broody to being more vocal, happy, more confident.
Suddenly I felt lighter and in sync with my body, the best rhythm of my life. I bowled extremely quick and accurate and gave the batsmen a hard time. When my bowling speed was checked it was at 130 kmph.

There isn't a coach or fitness trainer in the world who can have you raise your pace from 97kmph to 130 kmph in about a week. Even the greatest bowlers with 100s of wickets wouldn't be able to do it. Yet somehow your mind can".

I concur and believe we shouldn't reduce athletes to robots and over-expecting and projecting all our desires on them, which I feel hinders performance. 'Go for gold' is a outcome goal and not something to be emphasised before major events like the Olympics. Recall how Olympic medallist Simone Biles opted out at the Tokyo Olympics, citing the 'twisties', adding that it's immense pressure with millions of messages flooding in on social media. My mantra is to go enjoy the tournament and aim to beat your best, echoing Neeraj Chopra's Coach. 'Ja ke maze karo yaar' (meaning just go have fun) was the coach's message during the Tokyo Olympics, and as advised, he enjoyed the tournament and brought home the gold as a result.

At panel discussions and sports events that incessantly talk of our athletes lacking mental strength, I ask, are we supporting them as a sporting eco-system and, more importantly, providing a psychological safe space to aid their emergence? When we can hold the whole individual, performance will follow through. So, this has been my journey, to focus on the wholeness and well-being of the individual along with performance.

An international player winning a major title had said that compared to the war in his country, playing the finals was safer, which helped him stay focused on the task at hand rather than pressuring himself.

To conclude, helping athletes come to their reflective state is the key. My role is that of a catalyst to help them tap into their field of potential (FOP) and create magic—be it a junior or an Olympic medallist. May each of us find our niche to support athletes steeped in our roots and culture, as there really is no one way. In service of Indian sport—India always!

**Reflective Questions:**

- What brings you to your best state?
- When do you feel most prepared and open?
- Who and what supports you?
- What do you need to work upon?
- Are you ready to tap into your Field of Potential (FOP)?

## Note from Ashwini Nachappa

Sports psychology plays a crucial role in an athlete's performance, often making the difference between good and great. Unfortunately, this field has not always received the recognition it deserves. The mental aspect of sports is just as vital as physical training, as it influences mindset, focus, motivation, and resilience. By integrating mental training into their regimen, athletes can enhance their performance, set clear goals, and develop coping strategies for pressure and setbacks. My experiences as an early adopter of mental training way back in the 80s—when it was still an alien concept—truly inspired and motivated me, and ultimately gave me the results I was striving for. It was also incredibly pioneering, as it underscored the forward-thinking approach necessary to succeed in competitive sports. At my organisation, we have integrated mental training into our athletes' routine, and we've begun to notice the change in behaviour, attitude, and approach of our young athletes. The collaboration between athletes and coaches, supported by sports psychologists, fosters a holistic approach to training that can lead to remarkable performance outcomes. Hence, it is essential for sports psychology to receive the recognition it deserves, as it contributes significantly to the overall development of athletes.

**About Ashwini**

Ashwini Nachappa is a former international track and field athlete and Arjuna Award recipient, who represented India at the Asian Games, South Asian Federation Games, and World Championships. Over the course of her athletic career, she brought home multiple medals and inspired a generation of athletes. Beyond the track, Ashwini is a dedicated educationist, social worker, and actor. She founded a school to support youth development through education and currently serves as President of the Bangalore Urban District Athletics Association. Her multifaceted journey continues to influence and uplift the sporting and educational landscape in India.

## Note from Aditi Mutatkar & Darshan NK

Over the past few years, Aditi and Darshan have seen how mental health has remained an under-addressed aspect of athlete development in India. While the country is making strides in sports science, training methodologies, and performance analytics, psychological resilience and mental well-being are still not viewed as essential components of success.

As part of Simply Sport Foundation (SSF), we work through the Simply Smiles – Mental Health in Sport Initiative to bridge this critical gap. We don't just advocate for mental health awareness; we work actively on the ground to ensure that athletes, coaches, and support staff have access to structured interventions, education, and safe spaces to address psychological challenges in sport.

## The Need for Mental Health Support in Indian Sport

As individuals working closely with athletes, coaches, and sports organisations, we have seen how mental health issues are often misunderstood, stigmatised, or simply ignored. Athletes deal with immense pressure—performance expectations, injuries, financial constraints, and personal struggles—without a robust psychological support system in place. Some of the key gaps we have observed in the Indian sporting landscape include:

- Limited psychological literacy among coaches – Many coaches still focus primarily on technical and physical training, unaware of how psychological factors influence an athlete's mindset, motivation, and ability to handle setbacks.
- Lack of accessible mental health resources – While elite athletes have some level of access to sport psychologists, grassroots and mid-tier athletes struggle to find professional support.

- Fear of vulnerability – Athletes often hesitate to seek help, fearing judgment, reduced selection chances, or being labelled as "mentally weak."
- Neglect of women's mental health in sport – Unique challenges faced by female athletes, including menstrual health, gender bias, and self-doubt, are rarely discussed openly, leading to silent struggles.
- Parental pressure and lack of mental health awareness – Parents, though well-meaning, often unintentionally add to stress by prioritising results over process and well-being.

## Key Initiatives: Applying Psychological Principles to Sports

Through Simply Smiles, we have worked to not only build awareness but also embed psychological training into the sports ecosystem. Our approach is practical, based on years of field experience and real-time observations of what works in an Indian sporting context.

1. Coach Education: The First Line of Mental Health Support
   Through our work with hundreds of coaches across different levels of Indian sport, we've learned that coaches are the true game-changers in an athlete's mental well-being.

- As part of this initiative, we have developed structured workshops and training programs to help coaches:
  - Recognize early signs of mental distress in athletes.
  - Integrate psychological safety and emotional intelligence into their coaching approach.
  - Shift from a pressure-focused mindset to a support-driven coaching philosophy.

- Our Coaches' Mental Well-being Course, a first-of-its-kind online certification, is designed to provide practical tools that enable coaches to build resilient, motivated, and mentally strong teams.

Challenge: Many coaches resist discussing mental health due to traditional beliefs that "mental toughness" comes only from discipline and hard work. Opportunity: By integrating mental training seamlessly into their existing coaching methods, we've seen a positive shift where coaches now use psychological strategies to enhance performance rather than seeing them as separate from training.

2. Women in Sport: Mental Health, Menstrual Health, and Nutrition
   As a former national-level athlete, Aditi has personally experienced the silence and lack of resources around female athletes' psychological well-being.
   Conversations about self-doubt, body image, menstrual cycles, and mental fatigue are often brushed aside, leaving many young female athletes struggling alone.

- SSF has launched a Women in Sport initiative to address:
  - The link between mental health and menstrual health – How hormonal changes impact mood, confidence, and performance.
  - Gender-specific challenges in sport psychology – Managing societal expectations, self-doubt, and internalized pressure.
  - A tracking model for female athletes – Helping them monitor their well-being and adjust their training accordingly.
- This initiative will roll out in April 2025, combining online and offline tools for better athlete engagement.

Challenge: Many female athletes still hesitate to speak openly about mental health due to fear of appearing "weak."

Opportunity: By working with women coaches and former female athletes, we are normalizing these discussions and equipping them with the right tools to mentor young athletes effectively.

3. Athlete and Parent Engagement: A Holistic Approach

   One of the biggest realizations we have had in working with athletes is that their psychological environment is deeply influenced by their parents. Parents want the best for their children, but many struggle to balance encouragement with overwhelming pressure.

- Our Athlete Parent Support Module is designed to:
  - Help parents understand stress management, goal setting, and emotional resilience.
  - Conduct Focus Group Discussions (FGDs) to address parental concerns and create structured guidance.
  - Bridge the gap between athlete mental health needs and parental expectations.

Challenge: Many parents still believe "tough love" is the best approach for motivation. Opportunity: Educating parents about psychological support leads to healthier parent-athlete relationships, ultimately improving performance and well-being.

**SSF's Vision for the Future**

The mental health movement in Indian sport is just beginning, but we believe we are at a tipping point. At SSF, we are committed to driving real change by ensuring:

- Every athlete has access to mental health support.
- Coaches become advocates for psychological well-being.
- Women's mental health in sport receives the attention it deserves.
- Sporting organisations integrate mental training as a standard practice. Through continued partnerships, research, and education, we aim to reshape the Indian sporting culture where success is not just about medals and records but also about the mental well-being of athletes, coaches, and support staff.

**About Aditi**

Aditi Mutatkar is a five-time national badminton champion who represented India for over 16 years on the international circuit. A silver medalist in the mixed team event at the 2010 Commonwealth Games, she reached a career-high world ranking of 27 in 2008. She holds a Master's degree in Public Administration from the University of Texas and a Graduate Certificate in Public Policy from the Takshashila Institution. Aditi currently leads Athlete and Women initiatives at Simply Sport Foundation. Her experience informs her current work supporting athletes' holistic development.

**About Darshan**

Darshan NK is a seasoned sports management professional with over a decade of experience in India's sports industry. He currently serves as the Head of Programs and Fundraising at Simply Sport Foundation, where he leads initiatives aimed at developing grassroots sports and supporting athlete welfare. Darshan's prior roles include positions at Cure.Fit, XLR8 Indoor Sports Arena, and Lagardère Sports, where he focused on partnerships, talent scouting, and venue operations. His passion for sports development is evident through his involvement in major events like the London 2012 Olympics and the Davis Cup. An avid football enthusiast, Darshan is committed to creating meaningful pathways for Indian athletes to succeed on the global stage.

## Note from Dr. Chris Harwood

### Transferring what 'We know' into what 'They do': Closing the Know-Do Gap

#### Introduction

I am sometimes asked to talk about Talent Development Environments (TDEs) in my work, and one of the observations I have is how long it takes applied, scientific knowledge to translate into practice or impact in the field. I use Martindale and colleagues' (2005) guide on talent development to consider how much my experience of TDEs (and those of my practitioner peers) matches up with the holistic, long-term and collaborative components outlined by Martindale. Many of us are still talking 20 years later of the gaps; the developmental components that are missing or the elements that are paid lip service (e.g., the personal and life skills development of the young person). It's as if the research is being produced, and much more since (see Hauser et al., 2022), but the knowledge is not breaking through into actual improvements in environments. Someone is not listening, or we are not advocating enough; I imagine indeed there are many barriers and challenges, but I hope in India there is an opportunity to bridge the 'know-do' gap. In this case, it is sharing what we 'know' from applied science, and helping the implications to be what athletes, coaches, parents, and organisations actually 'do' day to day in sport.

#### Key Opportunities

There are several opportunities and requirements here from my experience in terms of practitioners.

Firstly, there is a need to start early, and that means recognising that the most enriching work in my view lies in youth sport environments. It requires practitioners to have very sound theoretical and applied knowledge of matters related to children, youth and families. An interest in positive youth development and life skills literature is important here in helping organisations bring more of a holistic focus to their athlete support.

Second, it means being able to understand and communicate the psychological demands of sport to parents and athletes in ways that capture their imagination and help them to appreciate the importance of psychological skills. Moreover, it means illustrating to and working with parents on ways that they can help nurture their child's athletic development and well-being. I have always believed that we can keep psychology quite straightforward and accessible through the 5Cs framework (Harwood, 2008; Harwood & Anderson, 2015)

Third, it means understanding wider sport science disciplines and illustrating to parents, coaches, and athletes how your wider knowledge of athletic development ties into your psychological role in helping the athlete to be disciplined and focused across other areas than simply mental skills (e.g., nutrition, physical training, sleep, injury prevention).

Finally, it means facilitating closer collaborations between parents and coaches so that communication is maximised, decision-making is well-informed, and key elements are well-coordinated for the child who is investing quite a bit of time in one sport activity.

All of these above features may be culturally interesting to reflect upon in an Indian context. Some may be more challenging goals or missions to complete for the practitioner in youth sport environments. However, sport psychology knowledge exists already to help athletes, coaches, parents, and organisations be the best they can be; it is much more a matter of organisations taking the time to listen to you with your 'wide knowledge' of this area and putting programmes together. It is imperative of course, as an emerging field in India, that you complete a postgraduate degree in sport psychology and train under supervision, but I believe the opportunities are there.

**About Dr. Chris**

Professor Chris Harwood is a renowned sport psychologist and Director of the Sport, Health and Performance Enhancement (SHAPE) Research Centre at Nottingham Trent University (NTU). With a distinguished career spanning over three decades, Chris has made significant contributions to the field of sport psychology, particularly in athlete development, wellbeing, and performance. His research focuses on the psychosocial aspects of youth sport and the integration of psychological principles into athletic environments. Chris has worked extensively with athletes, coaches, and parents to optimize performance and wellbeing, both in grassroots and elite sports settings. He has published over 160 journal articles and books, shaping the field of sport psychology through his work. In addition to his academic role, Chris has held leadership positions in sport psychology training and professional development, including serving as the lead psychologist for the National Tennis Centre and Nottingham Forest FC. His work continues to influence the future of sports psychology, focusing on creating supportive environments for young athletes and their families.

SECTION III

# ECOSYSTEM AND INTERPRETATION

*"Alone we can do so little; together we can do so much."*

**– Helen Keller**

# CRITICAL ROLE OF PLAY IN PEDAGOGY -

## PARTH PARASHER

Play-based pedagogy must be defined, structured, and universally integrated into the Indian school curriculum. This chapter outlines key concepts, the benefits of play for children, and practical applications of play-based pedagogy. It incorporates real-life examples and a case study from my work as a sports psychologist in India.

The significance of play extends beyond mere recreation. It is deeply intertwined with learning, creativity, and the holistic development of individuals. As we delve into its applications in pedagogy, it becomes evident that integrating play in important independent and functional to education is not a luxury but a necessity for fostering well-rounded individuals.

### Defining Pedagogy and Play

Pedagogy is the art and science of teaching, blending evidence-based practices with creative approaches to foster learning. Derived from the Greek words “paidos” (child) and “agogos” (leading), pedagogy embraces both cognitive and emotional dynamics of education.

Play transcends mere leisure; it’s a fundamental aspect of learning. Play engages children’s curiosity and enhances their problem-solving skills. It also fosters social and emotional development. Scholars like Piaget and Vygotsky have emphasized play as essential for experiential and collaborative learning. According to Vygotsky, play is pivotal in enabling children to perform at their "zone of proximal development," pushing them to explore beyond their current capabilities.

There are several benefits of Play in Learning. Play stimulates brain circuits linked to positive emotions, as evidenced by Jaak Panksepp's research.

Activities like pretend play enhance executive functions, such as goal setting, self-regulation, and creative problem-solving. Structured games, such as puzzles and strategy-based board games, encourage critical thinking and decision-making.

Play activates neural systems responsible for motivation and joy, creating a buffer against stress. Beyond its immediate enjoyment, it also nurtures by providing a safe and supportive space for children to express and regulate their emotions. Through role-playing scenarios, children practice empathy and develop coping mechanisms for real-life challenges. Moreover, play fosters essential social skills such as negotiation, collaboration, and conflict resolution. Shared activities encourage an understanding of social dynamics, while group play—such as team sports—— enhances communication, adaptability, and leadership.

Beyond its cognitive and emotional benefits, play also promotes physical fitness and motor skill development and encourages active lifestyles, combating sedentary behaviours and associated health risks.

During my interactions with club owners, directors, managers, coaches, educators, players, sport scientists, and health professionals in sport, I have observed several challenges and criticisms to deploying a play-based pedagogy. Firstly, critics of the play-based pedagogy argue that unrestricted play may lack clear learning outcomes. However, guided play bridges this gap by aligning activities with curricular goals. Teachers often need additional training to effectively implement structured play activities. Secondly, even children from well-off backgrounds in reputed schools lack access to enriching play experiences. Schools must address this by integrating play into public education systems and creating inclusive play environments. This can be done by ensuring the staff is physically literate (IPLA, 2014).

Seldom have I encountered critics who claim play detracts from literacy and numeracy. However, research shows that play enhances these skills by improving cognitive engagement and creating a positive attitude towards learning. In traditional education systems like those in India, play is often undervalued compared to academic rigor. Changing this mindset requires advocacy and awareness programs.

Ludic social constructivist pedagogical approach in Psychosocial skills training in India

"Play must always be in total agreement with the child as well as with his environment and cannot stand in isolation or be divorced from it; play will then be educative, serious, and meaningful. Through it, life becomes more relevant". - Fröbel (Liebschner,1993)

Over the past few years, I have had the opportunity to work with young athletes and students of diverse backgrounds. During my apprenticeship at a UK-based Premier League academy as a Sport Psychologist, I came across the 5Cs Psychosocial skills training framework (Harwood, 2008) conceptualised by Dr Chris Harwood, who also happened to be my supervisor at Loughborough University. The 5Cs framework encapsulated five broad psychological performance domains, such as Commitment (motivational),

Communication (interpersonal), Concentration (focus), Control (emotional regulation), and Confidence (self-beliefs) could be applied to profile and evaluate athletes using self-report and behavioural markers at the PL academy.

Structuring play into a Residential Academy Sport Psychology program, The 5Cs, based on an academy survey, were further classified into 15 standards (3 for each C). Each standard covered a distinct aspect of the psychological performance domain (e.g., in the commitment domain, standards were classified into goal setting competencies, monitoring intensity of effort, and pursuing optimal challenges). In the 5Cs curriculum, getting players to acknowledge and apply their teammates' qualities was one of the challenges that was identified and worked upon in a play-based setting. Play was structured in the academy classroom where I initiated the activity (e.g., building a marshmallow tower) and the players had the freedom to approach the task in various ways (Parasher, 2019). I maintained detailed observation notes and guided players to insights about themselves and their teammates.

The learning outcomes were structured in these sessions and were centred around increasing knowledge of self and others' psychological attributes. The players progressed to the football pitch where they played small-sided games and reflected on how they could use their qualities and others' qualities to achieve better tactical outcomes on the pitch.

During play the players embodied the understanding gained by physically 'acting it out' in accordance with their individual and collective goals. This approach paid dividends and delivered multiple positive outcomes for the academy. Many players who were limited by a didactic approach felt they could signify elite-level 5 Cs in play. Play was their fundamental medium of communication, and they felt they could express, or rather had been expressing all the while, but were only now being communicated with. This is in line with extant research, which suggests that play could be the language of the child no matter what the context (Beigi, 2020, pg.13).

Similar play activities were structured in the program for other C domains such as use of role-play to build empathy in the dressing room and improving self-regulation (e.g. when facing a camera and giving interviews during media training), using charades to bring attention to movement as a signifier, classroom games to improve reaction speed, divided attention tasks during games to improve focus, building a mindset Lego castle where each castle part represented a specific learning outcomes on growth and resiliency modules etc. (Parasher, 2019)

The results of employing a play-based pedagogy were positive. Players' learning outcomes increased, which were reflected in their performances on the pitch. Applying a play-based pedagogy ensured that the 5Cs were more than unidimensional signifiers for native Indian second language speakers. By embodying the Cs in classroom activities and on the pitch, the players reported several improved psychological outcomes such as high confidence, better self-regulation, improved self-assessment and goal-setting practices, high cohesion, and resilience. Coach knowledge, self-belief, educational and cultural contexts, competency, leadership styles, and communication strategies were significant moderators in the effectiveness of learning outcomes. These players went on to secure significant results against first academy teams of world-renowned clubs such as Manchester United, Arsenal, Southampton FC, Aston Villa FC, etc.

At the end of my time in Mumbai, the COVID pandemic ensured that players were restricted to their homes, due to which conducting play in a physical social setting was not possible. Although I was able to initiate work on constructing a digital play pedagogy for the academy, the unique set of challenges that presented themselves during the pandemic made it difficult to focus on applying the same within the academy. Future 5Cs research focused on optimising digital play approaches to improve psychological outcomes amongst students.

Although there have been several Institutional constraints and moderators (such as the scarcity of highly qualified coaches, cultural scenario, schedule constraints, organisational goals and expectations) that have hindered the applications play-based pedagogy (Leather, Harper & Obee, 2021), I have undertaken interviews, workshops and assessments to adopt the pedagogy at my current workplace- a Residential School in Rajasthan awarded the 2024 "Best School promoting Sport in the Country" by Federation of Indian Chambers of Commerce and Industry.

The skills learnt under the 5Cs program are transferable and can be applied in the classroom and boarding-house setting, promoting strengths and assets development through cultural activities as well. Through play (Panksepp,1998), students learn to interpret and respond to social cues such as facial feedback and body language (communication)—something less emphasized in traditional teacher-led instruction. Through role play, children enhance empathy and broaden their understanding of perspectives beyond their own (commitment). It also allows them to explore moral decision-making by testing their actions in real-life scenarios and refining their sense of right and wrong.

The 5Cs (Harwood, 2008) developed through play can lead to a greater sense of competence and self-assurance outside the classroom (confidence).

Another advantage of employing a play-based pedagogy in class is that it instils deeper experiential understanding of social hierarchies (Kagan and Lowenstein, 2004). Students are learning to manage conflicts and improve self-regulation during play, which is essential to prepare them for life beyond the classroom (concentration and control).

Reflecting on personal experiences: Play pedagogy in Sports Psychology Training During my tenure at elite football academies in Maharashtra and Karnataka and at boarding schools in Assam and Rajasthan, I adapted psychosocial skills training to Indian cultural contexts using play-based methods.

I faced several challenges in implementing a top-down skill-ed program like the 5Cs, that which can be mainly condensed into three themes- language barriers, lack of awareness, and cultural differences. Coaches struggled to communicate theoretical concepts, and their familiarity with play-based methods was limited.

At an elite football academy in Mumbai, we figured that guided play would help bridge this gap. I implemented fun and engaging activities like designing and constructing a mini tower, which encouraged teamwork and communication, creating perceptual constraints to highlight selective attention to sensory stimuli, conducting scanning activities in the classroom to showcase the neurocognitive aspects of visual exploratory behaviour on the pitch (span, frequency etc.)

We used role play and other empathy-building exercises in the dressing room, which improved interpersonal trust and communication. Some of the outcomes we observed were - players developed psychological resilience and cohesion. The academy achieved significant results against globally renowned teams, including Manchester United and Arsenal. Players reported improved self-confidence and communication skills, highlighting the transformative power of structured play.

With support from the coaching and technical staff, I also developed a holistic Psychosocial Skills Training Manual for football coaches. The sessions were age-appropriate, considering cognitive development, technical learning progression, coaching styles, performance schemas, and physical constraints.

1. Table: Play vs. Traditional Learning:
   Strategies for Implementation in Indian Schools
   - Integrate play into daily lessons, linking it with academic objectives. Develop a structured play-based curriculum that aligns seamlessly with existing subjects
   - Equip educators with skills to facilitate guided play. Workshops and certifications can help teachers incorporate play into lesson plans effectively.
   - Design environments catering to diverse abilities and interests. Examples include sensory play areas for children with special needs.
   - Host workshops for parents to emphasize the value of play.

   Collaborate with local organisations to create community play days.
   - Advocate for policies that prioritize play-based learning in educational reform initiatives.
   - Implement the SMILES framework in Coaching

## Conclusion

This chapter demonstrated how play-based pedagogy fosters cognitive, social, and emotional growth in children. Through real-world examples and a case study, we saw its practical impact on learning and development.

By embedding structured play into Indian schools, we can move beyond rigid academics to create engaging, skill-building environments where students thrive—not just in school, but in life.

# SLEEP AND SPORT IN THE INDIAN CONTEXT -

## DR. AYAN MRUGANK MERCHANT

Sleep is an important independent and functional life process that is basic to all living organisms. My encounter with sleep began four years ago when I applied for my PhD at the University of Glasgow. My knowledge of sleep at that time was limited in scope. I understood the basic importance of sleep to our health, knowing that it is an essential life function. I had some basic experience with sleep, with coaches asking me to address the detrimental effects of a lack of sleep on performance associated with social media usage and watching various late-night sporting events in India. However, as every researcher will inform us, we never truly understand a subject until we start working on it and realise how much we don't know about it; eventually, it becomes a passionate, deep dive into a subject that is still quite unknown and keeps expanding.

Sleep is essential to healthy living. Its intricate effects on our physical and mental health are far more extensive than anyone can imagine. We all need sleep; the average individual sleeps 6-8 hours per night. When we sleep, we go through five stages, including Rapid Eye

Movement and Non-Rapid Eye Movement. These stages make up the sleep cycle of our circadian rhythm.

The circadian rhythm is what we call our 'BODY CLOCK'. This body clock functions over 24 hours and manages many of our daily schedules and bodily functions, including digestion, body temperature, and hormonal functioning. It works on environmental cues or the lack of them to determine our daily schedules. Special cells in our retinas process light and inform us whether it's day or night, determining our sleep-wake schedule. Imagine that you are stuck in a dark cave without information about day or night. You would still feel hungry at a particular time. You would feel sleepy at a specific time and wake up as well. The circadian rhythm determines how we function. As we are not stuck in a cave right now (even though it seemed like that during COVID), we can confidently say that daylight is the most significant influencer of the circadian rhythm.

Over the past few years, numerous studies have focused on the importance of sleep in sports. Although the topic of sleep is expansive, preliminary studies on sleep and sports consist of interventions and assessments based on the Western perspective. In this chapter, I aim to expand on the importance of sleep in sports, how sleep affects well-being, health, and performance, and

various strategies used to improve sleep with an emphasis on the Indian perspective.

## Why is sleep important for Athletes?

Sleep is a universal function of all multicellular organisms and is a biological requirement for life, similar to the need for food, water, and air. Sleep plays an important role in health and well-being, consisting of and affecting multiple neurobiological and physiological systems such as metabolism, cognition, performance, immune function, and social and emotional regulation. Therefore, sleep plays a crucial role in an athlete's life. Compared to non-athletes, evidence shows athletes tend to have lower sleep quality and less sleep duration (6.5-.6.7 hours a night) realising this, more and more athletes are actively focusing on the importance of sleep to aid Physical Recovery and Performance, Mental Health and Cognitive Function, Immune System Support and Injury Prevention, and Neuromuscular Skills.

Let's do a quick activity: Imagine that you are an elite tennis player preparing for Wimbledon. You have had a restless night and are facing the first of a series of challenging matches with the best of the best in the world. Imagine yourself feeling groggy, not well-rested, and stressed all at the same time. The lack of sleep overwhelms you with the prospect of playing in such an important international event. You would struggle to maintain composure. As the match goes on, you find your reactions slow and impair your ability to make spontaneous decisions. This can be disastrous, especially in a sport like tennis. You feel angry, frustrated, and upset at yourself. Now imagine a month of sleep deprivation. Over time, this leads to a significant decline in mental and cognitive health and your ability to face difficult challenges, especially in competitive sports.

The increasing pressure on athletes to train longer, faster, and higher to provide optimum performance can lead to physical stress and an overload on one's physiological functioning. In India, additional stressors such as pollution, varied climate, and travel can compromise an athlete's immunity. This is an occupational hazard that can be tackled with adequate restorative sleep.

What are the factors that can affect Sleep in Indian Athletes?

In my early training programs, I conducted sessions on good sleep practices for teenagers who often stayed up late watching TV. To my surprise, the sessions highlighted how biological changes, sociocultural norms, and technology can complicate sleep issues and how we can address them.

Indian athletes face numerous sleep challenges that impact performance and recovery, which include cultural factors, lack of awareness, inconsistent schedules, limited resources, overtraining, excessive use of electronics, environmental factors, travel fatigue, and economic constraints.

Traditionally in India, sleep and rest are considered signs of weakness and unproductiveness. The culture of working through tiredness and exhaustion is celebrated, leading to negative behavioural patterns resulting in overtraining and neglect of both physical and mental health. All too often, we witness young athletes in a high-performance facility with long training hours and constant practice to try and ensure perfection. Often grappling with performance pressure, the concept of rest or recovery is frowned upon, and as a result, the athletes train out of guilt and neglect sleep. Struggling with chronic sleep deprivation, the athlete struggles both physically and mentally with deteriorating performance.

Another significant learning for me was how athletes manage academics, family commitments, and societal expectations with training within the Indian context. Balancing social events and training sessions can create enormous friction, leading to late nights and insufficient recovery periods. Especially for a young student-athlete, it can become daunting to train and engage in normal teenage activities such as meeting friends, attending events, and celebrating festivals. Napping is the most commonly used tool to aid recovery. However, that can also be viewed as lazy or unproductive behaviour and thus avoided, leading to insufficient rest. There is a need to create more awareness of the importance of sleep, along with the more visible aspects of performance, such as nutrition, training, diet, and fitness.

One of the most common complaints athletes have is their intense and difficult schedules. Competitive athletes travel constantly due to the increasing number of tournaments and competitions. As a result, they face issues like jet lag and environmental pressures, such as noise, light, humidity, crowding, and heat, resulting in disrupted training schedules and insufficient sleep. When speaking to athletes, the most common feedback was tight tournament schedules and a lack of adequate transportation facilities, which led to fatigue, impacting performance. Due to training demands and a lack of facilities, athletes often miss short naps, leading to exhaustion and burnout.

Another big challenge to sleep deprivation is the technological changes that have occurred in the last few decades. Everyone is guilty of spending time on their phones, especially at night. After all, who doesn't love a doom scroll? Due to stress, demanding lifestyles, and schedules, we spend our nights on our phones or computers. Athletes are no different; like all of us, they also spend a significant amount of time using electronic devices before bedtime. Given their packed and difficult schedules, it is not surprising. However, using electronic devices has been found to disrupt sleep cycles, delaying sleep onset and reducing sleep quality.

Let's try another exercise: Picture yourself at the gym doing deadlifts. The barbell is in front of you, and you've loaded it with 10kg weights. After your first lift, you feel it's insufficient, so you add another 10 kg. You find it still too light and keep adding weights until it becomes unmanageable or could potentially cause injury. This illustrates the effects of sleep deprivation. A couple of nights with poor sleep often go unnoticed, and many of us have experienced this. Balancing early morning training and family, school, homework, socialising, and sleep, the weight on our schedules can feel overwhelming, making it easy to let sleep take a backseat, but regularly sacrificing sleep can adversely impact our performance.

## How can these factors be addressed?

As sleep and napping are crucial for optimising sports performance and recovery, we must identify and address obstacles effectively to sustain performance while ensuring health and well-being.

Cultural and Social Factors: As a psychologist, I have always maintained that a healthy balance is required between our traditional lifestyles and an athlete's schedule demands. How often do we ask ourselves, "What does this athlete need"? Families and communities need to be aware of athletes' requirements and ensure they have adequate time for rest and recovery. Athletes often balance their sports, academics, and family needs, which can compromise sleep due to guilt and fear of non-performance. We all need to readjust our expectations and agree that prioritising athletes' sleep and rest is essential.

The narrative that sleep equates to being lazy or unproductive needs to be changed. A more cohesive culture focusing on how sleep can aid an athlete's discipline, productivity, and performance is essential. The role of the family and community is key to changing this narrative. Educating parents, family, and community members about the importance of sleep for an athlete can help create a supportive environment for healthier sleep and athlete performance.

Academic Balance: Academic success is considered essential for an individual's future. Many young athletes face pressure to perform academically and in their sports, leading to sleep deprivation and affecting their education and performance. Athletes, parents, and educational institutions must create a plan with effective time management and goals to help balance an athlete's sporting and educational commitments. Providing flexible schedules, extra classes or tutoring, counselling, and creating an environment that places equal importance on academic successes and sporting aspirations leads to a healthy balance between both.

Environmental Challenges, Impact, and Solutions: Athletes deal with environmental concerns like noise, humidity, crowding, and temperature changes. In parts of India, loud noise, pollution levels, and extreme heat and humidity can be challenging for athletes, making them vulnerable to illnesses and health concerns. I often request that athletes travel with their pillows and blankets if it's feasible or use white noise machines (which are even available on their phones now). Air purifiers and air conditioners can also help mitigate some of these issues in highly polluted areas. Athletes, coaches, support staff, and administrators must work together to create an optimal sleeping environment to address these challenges. Similarly, organising good travel plans and comfortable accommodation is often overlooked and needs to be addressed by parents, academies, and coaches.

Use of Technology: In recent years, the development of tools and technology has helped us monitor sleep and improve sleeping habits. These tools are greatly beneficial for athletes who need sufficient sleep duration and quality. Conversely, screen exposure before bedtime can affect our sleep cycle and disrupt sleep. Creating routines to limit screen time, reducing exposure to blue light, and using apps and wearable technology can lead to a healthier lifestyle and improve sleep schedules for better rest and recovery. With younger athletes, I offer a comprehensive approach, including wind-down routines and engaging in passive activities. If things take a more serious turn, sitting down and creating a plan with parents, coaches, and the athletes is important.

Economic considerations and cost-effective tools: In rural areas, the lack of resources can lead to difficulties in sleeping environments and, at times, access to sleep-related tools. Therefore, it is important to create awareness programs on the importance of sleep and use cost-effective tools to aid sleeping conditions, such as comfortable bedding, natural remedies, eye masks, and earplugs, which can help athletes get enough rest. In India, these aspects might be difficult to address given that athletes, at times, are not used to these "foreign methods". In such cases, I learnt early on that it is important to use the available resources and methods that they find useful and simple, e.g., curtains can block out excess light and utilise space effectively for sleep (especially in smaller homes or while travelling), can work wonders.

Importance of Napping: Naps can be an effective recovery method and are one of the most powerful tools in an athlete's arsenal. In conversation with Duraflex, Virat Kohli spoke about using strategic napping techniques to combat the late-night match schedules and ensure he is well-rested before his games. Planning naptimes of 20-30 minutes in the morning or early afternoon has been known to help improve performance. Creating a schedule to integrate naps into rest and recovery is important and ensures the athlete is not sleepy during match times. Naps and rest can help athletes maintain their gruelling schedules, travel, jetlag, and recovery from competitions.

**What therapies and strategies are used?**

Various techniques address sleep-related difficulties, including education, psychotherapeutic interventions, nutrition, and sleep aids. These methods include Cognitive Behavioural Therapy for Insomnia (CBT-I), Sleep Hygiene Training, Relaxation Techniques, Mindfulness Meditation, Strategic Napping and Sleep Scheduling, Bright Light Therapy, Nutritional Interventions, Sleep and Stress Management Counselling, and, of course, Sleep Aids and Supplements and can offer various benefits to athletes depending on their individual sleep patterns and can be conducted under supervision either independently or in combination.

Using the above techniques helps athletes adopt healthier lifestyle habits, leading to better physiological and mental health, which is essential for optimal performance. However, it must be noted that every individual has different sleep-wake cycles, so one should take a personalised approach based on what works best.

**What does Indian sport need at the moment?**

In India, coaches, athletes, and support teams have become increasingly aware of the role of sleep in their performance and training, which is motivating, but there needs to be a significant change in adopting good sleep practices, and a more holistic approach is required to sustain athletic performance and good health.

Education on the importance of sleep and shifting cultural perceptions is vital for athlete health and performance. Collaborating with sleep experts, psychologists, doctors, and other professionals is essential to develop strategies and address sleep issues, making these resources accessible at grassroots levels, not just for high-performance athletes.

Various scientific tools and technologies have been found useful to athletes for sleep tracking and optimal performance. However, most available tools have a more Western perspective and language barriers, with low applicability for the Indian population. While some global tools have been adapted for local use, there is a significant need to develop homegrown assessment tools and technology that address our cultural needs, resulting in better-tailored assessments and outcomes.

While Indian athletes are working to make sleep an important part of their skill set, further development, including education, access to resources, and better sleep practices across Indian sports, is essential to create high-performance and professional athletes and also safeguard their physical and mental health.

**Reflection & Exercises Section**

1. What are your current views on sleep in the sporting world?
2. What are the key points or concepts in this chapter?
3. How can athletes develop healthy sleep habits?
4. Can changing sleep patterns be challenging in the Indian environment?
5. What area of sleep can be addressed most significantly?
6. How would you incorporate sleep into an athlete's routine?

# IT TAKES A VILLAGE TO RECOVER FROM INJURIES: THE ROLE OF PSYCHOSOCIAL SUPPORT IN INJURY REHABILITATION –

## VAISHALI CHAUDHARY & DR. CHAITANYA SRIDHAR

In our work with athletes, we have often been struck by the fact that while we invest heavily in physical rehabilitation post-injury, the mental scars are sometimes overlooked. We frequently find ourselves questioning how we, as professionals, can better address the psychological side of injury recovery. It is this curiosity, combined with a deep sense of responsibility towards the athletes, that has driven us to explore this topic in greater depth.

A weightlifter faced recurrent injuries yet remained dedicated to returning to the sport. Navigating emotional highs and lows—from fear of losing her form to feelings of isolation and frustration— she demonstrated extraordinary psychological resilience throughout. Her journey underscores the critical importance of mental support during injury recovery.

For many athletes, more than the injury and recovery itself, the greater challenge lay in helping their coaches, teammates, and the broader sporting ecosystem understand the emotional toll they endure. An interpersonal shift where their parents and coaches, and other support staff can provide them with a supportive environment, can actually help athletes be self-compassionate and patient with themselves as they navigate the long and demanding journey of rehabilitation.

## Socio-Cultural Influences on Perception of Injury and Recovery

Injury is an inevitable part of an athlete's career, but the way athletes respond to it—physically, psychologically, and emotionally—can vary widely. These responses are influenced by a complex web of factors, including the sociocultural context in which the athlete is embedded. Cultural values, societal expectations, and community norms shape not only an athlete's perception of injury but also their approach to recovery. For instance, in countries like India, where mental toughness is often equated with physical endurance, seeking help for psychological or emotional distress might be seen as a sign of weakness. This cultural framework can lead athletes to underutilize support systems, both in terms of physical rehabilitation and mental health care.

We would like to share a particular case of a young male weightlifter from Punjab in northern India (using the name Raj for this example). Raj sustained a serious back injury during training but delayed seeking medical help due to the cultural expectation that an athlete should push through pain. In Raj's community, resilience is often measured by one's ability to endure hardship

without complaint, and vulnerability is seen as a flaw. Even his coach didn't appreciate athletes taking breaks and encouraged Raj to continue training using a belt to support his back. As a result, Raj hid his pain from the physiotherapist and delayed consulting the sports medicine doctor. It was only

> Injury itself is not the problem. How we perceive it and process it makes all the difference. This perspective is shaped by our personality, thought patterns, and the people around us. With the right mindset and support, an injury can become a catalyst for growth rather than just a setback.

after a few months of pushing himself like this that he finally told his coach that the pain was unbearable, who then advised him to visit the doctor. By this time, the minor pain had developed into a serious injury, and Raj was advised to undergo rehabilitation and rest for at least six months. This is when he first came to the psychologist and shared how upset and stressed he was about being out of training for such a long time. He expressed feelings of guilt for not speaking to the physiotherapist and doctor earlier. During the psychology sessions, it gradually became clear that Raj's reluctance to fully commit to rehabilitation was deeply rooted in societal pressures. He feared being judged by his peers, coach, and even his family for appearing weak.

Research supports the idea that societal pressures can significantly impact an athlete's emotional well-being during recovery. For example, Bianco, Malo, and Orlick (1999) found that athletes who feel pressured to quickly return to competition often experience heightened anxiety and frustration during their rehabilitation.

> True recovery requires not only resilience from the athlete but also a supportive ecosystem—coaches, parents, support staff and teammates—who understand and address the emotional toll. It is this interplay of mental strength and interpersonal support that forms the foundation of this chapter.

In Raj's case, this pressure was exacerbated by cultural expectations, making it difficult to focus on recovery without the looming fear of disappointing his community. By addressing these cultural influences in the psychology sessions, we reframed recovery not as a sign of weakness but as an essential part of an athlete's journey. Raj began to see rehabilitation as an opportunity to build resilience, both physically and mentally.

## Navigating the Psychological Challenges of Injury

For many athletes, sports is more than just an activity; they are central to their identity, social connection, and future aspirations. When an injury disrupts their training, it impacts not only their physical capabilities but also their sense of self, personal goals, and daily routines. This emotional turmoil can be as challenging as physical pain, as athletes confront a sudden interruption to their athletic journey.

In many cases, athletes experience emotional responses similar to the grieving process described by Kubler-Ross, which includes stages of denial, anger, bargaining, depression, and acceptance. Initially, there's usually a denial of the severity of the injury, where the athlete downplays its impact, often attempting to continue training or competing. Anger may follow, directed at themselves, the circumstances, or even their support team, as they grapple with feelings of helplessness. Bargaining might manifest in thoughts such as, "If I just rest for a week, I'll be back," and some of them even try to rush through the rehab phase. For some, depression sets in as they confront the injury's full impact. Athletes may feel sadness or hopelessness as they face the uncertainty of their return to sport.

What's crucial to note is that these responses are not limited to non-elite athletes pushing to reach higher levels. Many elite athletes, too, feel the pressure to continue training despite pain, believing it's necessary for performance. In our work, we have seen many athletes rely on temporary solutions, like tape or pain sprays, to complete a performance, only to regret it when minor injuries progress into severe ones.

As a society, we often overlook the emotional and psychological consequences of injuries, partly because emotions are undervalued in the Indian context. Mental health support is still seen as either irrelevant or a quick fix by many athletes and coaches in India. This mindset can lead to neglect of the psychological challenges that athletes face post-injury, including heightened anxiety, depression, and stress.

Injured athletes who feel cut off from their teammates or sport may also experience a loss of social identity, further intensifying their sense of grief and loss. For this reason, we usually suggest athletes stay connected to their training environment by passively attending the training sessions. Also, another intervention we use is to make them observe training sessions and visualize techniques that other athletes are practicing.

This helps athletes mentally engage with their sport, even if they are not physically active. Visualization thus becomes an important mental skill, offering the athletes a sense of accomplishment and connection to their athletic identity.

Addressing emotional responses is critical to ensuring athletes' successful recovery. This is where mindset coaching as part of the sport psychology sessions has proved to be an essential component of injury rehabilitation. As sport psychologists, we provide a space for athletes to work through their feelings of loss, anger, and frustration. Additionally, we also emphasize focusing on what they have lost to what they can control in the present. For example, we guide athletes to reframe negative thought patterns, replacing catastrophic thinking ("I'll never get back to where I was") with more constructive, goal-oriented thoughts ("This is an opportunity to strengthen other aspects of my game"). This focus on the 'here and now' aids in helping them build a more process-oriented mindset in the long term.

For athletes who develop a fear of re-injury, acceptance and commitment therapy (ACT) can be a valuable approach. Recently, while working with a competitive swimmer, we focused on how her fear of a potential re-injury was holding her back from engaging fully in rehabilitation. Together, we worked on accepting that, while injury is an inherent risk in sports, dwelling on that fear wasn't helping her move forward. Embracing this reality allowed the athlete to redirect her focus to the daily rehabilitation efforts, ultimately helping her feel more motivated and optimistic about returning to sport.

Furthermore, we also help athletes reconnect with their identity beyond sport. A lot of Indian athletes take up sports to avoid studies, and their whole focus shifts only to sports. Thus, they see their worth as linked exclusively to their athletic performance. So, when injury occurs, they feel like it is a personal failure. Through psychology sessions, we encourage athletes to explore other aspects of their identity and personal strengths, which provides them with a sense of purpose and motivation outside of sport. This broader perspective helps foster psychological flexibility, which is crucial during the often long and arduous rehabilitation process.

### Financial Concerns and Long-Term Career Anxiety

For many athletes in India, sports serve as a direct pathway to stable government employment through sports quotas. An injury, however, jeopardizes not only their athletic aspirations but also their anticipated job security, amplifying their financial stress and career anxiety. Research highlights how financial instability intensifies distress, with injured athletes often experiencing heightened anxiety, depression, and uncertainty about their future.

One such case that I've come across is that of a wrestler. She was preparing for job trials and sustained a severe elbow dislocation just before the trial day. This setback was devastating, as securing that job was vital to her future.

Although the athlete eventually recovered through surgery and returned to her sport, her age now limits the options to reapply for the same position, leading to periods of self-doubt and worry. In our sessions, we worked on rebuilding her confidence and providing consistent emotional support. Together, we also explored alternative career options so that the athlete could feel a sense of control over her future beyond wrestling.

In this case, as well as others, we have often observed that career-related stress is especially prevalent in athletes whose lives are deeply intertwined with sports, as many depend on these careers as their primary, and often sole, source of livelihood. For most Indian athletes like the one mentioned above, a common question looms: What will I do if I can't return to sport? This is an anxiety felt across backgrounds, but it's particularly severe for those coming from economically weaker sections, where sports is often the only pathway to financial stability. Parents, seeing this path, often push their children into sports early, viewing it as a "make-or-break" opportunity to secure their future. Unfortunately, without other vocational or academic skills to fall back on, young athletes feel trapped, as if their entire future hinges on each game or training session.

Addressing these challenges requires a cultural shift. Parents must be educated on the importance of holistic development, emphasizing academic and vocational skills alongside sports. Sports organisations and government programs can play a role by mandating basic education and offering skill development initiatives. These steps would provide athletes with an alternate career options, reducing the pressure of singular reliance on sports.

Athletic talent development environments model, adapted from Henriksen et al. (2010a)

Family support is particularly crucial during times of crisis. Parents and loved ones who foster resilience and encourage long-term planning can help athletes navigate setbacks with patience and confidence.

Holistic psychological interventions involving coaches and parents of athletes that address both emotional recovery and career planning have been shown to be highly beneficial. Wadey et al. (2011), for instance, found that recovery outcomes improve significantly when athletes feel supported both emotionally and in planning for their futures.

## Group Therapy: A Novel Approach to Injury Rehabilitation

Group therapy and support groups are an under-researched yet promising aspect of the injury rehabilitation process. These settings provide athletes with a space to share their experiences, frustrations, and triumphs with others who understand the unique challenges of athletic recovery. The shared nature of these sessions fosters a reciprocal support system where athletes at different stages of recovery can both offer and receive insight.

We observed this firsthand in a group session with athletes in various phases of their rehabilitation. The camaraderie and shared experiences helped alleviate the feelings of isolation that often accompany injuries. For instance, Clement and Shannon (2011) found that athletes who engaged in peer support groups experienced reduced anxiety and an increased sense of motivation compared to those who only received individual counselling. Encouraged by these findings, we aim to build more such groups to provide structured injury support to athletes.

Beyond group therapy, we have also implemented a 'buddy system,' where each athlete was paired with a peer responsible for checking in on them and informing the psychologist when necessary. This approach ensured consistent, peer-driven support, often surpassing the availability of professional support staff. Our firsthand experiences with these methods have reinforced their benefits, which is why we advocate for their inclusion in the broader rehabilitation framework.

Group settings can also facilitate "meaning-making" within a relational context, allowing athletes to validate their struggles through shared narratives. By framing their injuries as part of a broader journey rather than an isolated setback, athletes may develop a more resilient outlook. Carron and Brawley (2013) emphasize that meaning-making is a crucial component of psychological recovery, as it enables individuals to reframe adverse events in ways that foster resilience.

Additionally, incorporating family members and coaches into the rehabilitation process can significantly enhance the effectiveness of group therapy. Families serve as primary sources of emotional and logistical support for injured athletes, while coaches play a pivotal role in setting realistic expectations, fostering motivation, and creating a supportive environment. Integrating these key figures into group therapy sessions provides an opportunity for all parties to align their understanding of the athlete's recovery journey, fostering open communication and reducing misunderstandings.

For instance, parents participating in group sessions can gain deeper insights into the psychological challenges their children face during injury recovery.

This understanding enables them to provide constructive support without adding undue pressure. Similarly, coaches can learn how to adapt their communication and training strategies to better accommodate the athlete's evolving physical and emotional needs.

Mixed support groups, comprising athletes, parents, coaches, and support staff, offer a unique relational dynamic that deepens the healing process. These groups serve as platforms for shared storytelling, empathy-building, and collective problem-solving. Athletes can voice their progress and frustrations, while parents and coaches contribute their perspectives, fostering mutual understanding and encouragement.

A real-life example highlights the impact of such an approach. An athlete struggling with self-doubt about returning to their previous level of performance confided in the psychologist. Recognizing the importance of external reinforcement, the psychologist conveyed these concerns to the coach, who then reassured the athlete, without revealing their prior conversation, of their belief in the athlete's abilities, regardless of the injury. This seemingly small intervention led to a renewed sense of motivation, as the physiotherapist observed increased adherence to the rehabilitation plan following this conversation.

By integrating athletes, parents, coaches, and staff into a unified support system, a more holistic approach to injury recovery emerges. This method not only addresses the athlete's psychological well-being but also equips their support network with the necessary tools to sustain progress long after formal rehabilitation has ended.

## Concluding Thoughts

Injury recovery for athletes is far more than a solo journey; it is profoundly shaped by the presence and actions of their broader support network. This chapter has tried to highlight that while individual resilience and mindset are essential, an athlete's ecosystem—coaches, family, teammates, and mental health professionals—play an equally crucial role in navigating the emotional, financial, and identity-related challenges that injuries bring. By fostering a supportive and empathetic environment, this network can empower athletes to make meaning from their experiences, maintain their motivation, and visualize their path forward, even in the face of uncertainty.

**Exercise: Let's create an Athlete Support Plan!**

Think of an athlete you know has faced an injury at some point in their career. Imagine you're helping to create a holistic support plan to guide them through the psychological and emotional aspects of injury recovery. Answer the following questions to build a framework for this plan.

Who are the key people in this athlete's life who can provide support?

Identify one emotion you think this athlete might experience.

Think of a few strategies that could help the athlete deal with this emotion.

Think of two positive statements that the athlete can use for positive self-talk and can help them to stay motivated.

# MOULDING THE INNER CIRCLE -

KEERTHANA SWAMINATHAN & MAURELLE D'SA

In the world of sports, the psychological aspects of training are as fundamental as the physical, especially for young athletes in grassroots settings. Yet, the role of a sports psychologist is often misunderstood or oversimplified. Many view it as limited to enhancing performance through psychological skill training or addressing mental health concerns in a clinical context. While these are critical components, they represent only a fraction of what sports psychology entails. At its core, the role of a sports psychologist extends to shaping the very culture and ecosystem that surrounds the athlete, ensuring that the environment itself becomes a source of psychological safety, resilience, and growth.

Athletes do not exist in isolation. Their performance, well-being, and long-term development are deeply influenced by the relationships and environments they are part of—whether it's the interaction with coaches, the expectations from parents, or the dynamics within a team. Gabor Maté's insights on trauma and the mind-body connection emphasize how unresolved emotional stress within these systems can manifest physically, impacting both performance and mental health. For young athletes, psychological safety in their environment—knowing that they can express vulnerabilities, navigate failures, and seek support without judgment—becomes essential. Without it, even the most talented athletes may falter under pressure or carry hidden emotional burdens that undermine their potential.

Stephen Porges' Polyvagal Theory reinforces the importance of safety and connection. Porges highlights how the nervous system's perception of safety allows individuals to remain calm, engaged, and open to learning, while environments perceived as threatening trigger survival responses like fear and withdrawal. For athletes, this means their ability to train, adapt, and compete is directly tied to how secure they feel in their surroundings. Coaches, parents, and support staff play pivotal roles in co-regulating these emotional states with the athlete, either fostering a sense of safety or inadvertently contributing to stress and fear. The sports psychologist, in turn, acts as the architect of these interactions, equipping stakeholders with the tools and insights to create emotionally attuned environments.

Moreover, cultural context adds another layer of complexity. Geert Hofstede's work on cultural dimensions sheds light on how India's collectivist values and hierarchical structures shape relationships in grassroots sports academies.

While these cultural traits can foster discipline and loyalty, they can also create environments where athletes are hesitant to speak up, challenge authority, or express vulnerability. The sports psychologist's role here is to navigate these cultural dynamics, leveraging their strengths while addressing their limitations to cultivate psychological safety. By working with the inner circle—coaches, parents, and support staff—sports psychologists help bridge cultural gaps, encouraging open communication and mutual trust.

Fletcher and Sarkar's research on resilience further underscores the connection between environment and athlete development.

Resilience, often seen as an individual trait, is in fact co-created within environments that balance high challenges with high support. Grassroots academies, as the first formal systems shaping young athletes, have the responsibility to foster resilience not just through training drills but by creating ecosystems that build confidence, adaptability, and emotional strength. Sports psychologists are instrumental in this process, helping design systems and interactions that promote both performance excellence and psychological well-being.

Thus, the role of a sports psychologist is far more expensive than often assumed. It is not confined to individual interventions or mental health crises; it involves actively shaping the cultural and relational ecosystems surrounding the athlete. Whether through educating coaches on psychological literacy, guiding parents to adopt supportive behaviours, or fostering collaboration among multidisciplinary support teams, the sports psychologist ensures that psychological safety becomes a cornerstone of the athlete's environment.

This, in turn, impacts not only performance but also the long-term mental well-being of the athlete.

This chapter explores how grassroots sports academies in India can integrate these principles to mould the inner circle, transforming the athlete's immediate ecosystem into a source of strength and support. By emphasizing the interconnectedness of psychological safety, cultural awareness, and collaborative relationships, it aims to provide a blueprint for academies to nurture resilient, confident, and well-rounded athletes. The goal is not just to train athletes to perform but to equip them with the tools to thrive—on and off the field.

## Key Pillars in Fostering a Psychologically Supportive Environment

1. Mental Health literacy as a cornerstone
   Mental health literacy forms the bedrock of a psychologically supportive environment, empowering coaches and support staff to better understand,
   identify and address the psychological needs of athletes. This goes beyond recognizing overt signs of distress; it encompasses an awareness of the nuanced spectrum of mental health as proposed by Henriksen and colleagues.

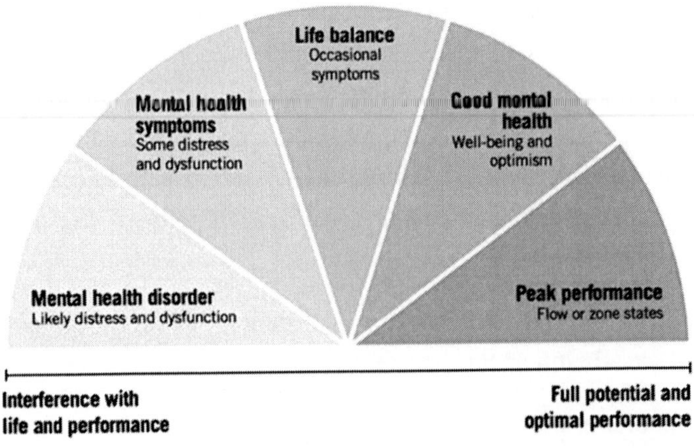


**Figure 1**

Henriksen's mental health spectrum illustrates that athletes exist on a continuum that spans mental health disorders, subclinical symptoms, balance, good mental health, and peak performance (Figure 1). This understanding allows coaches to see mental health not as a binary state of "healthy" or "unhealthy," but as a dynamic process influenced by various factors, including stress, competition, support systems, coping strategies, and life circumstances.

For instance, an athlete recovering from an injury may fall into a **"reacting" or "struggling" state**, experiencing self-doubt, frustration, and reduced confidence without meeting clinical criteria for anxiety or depression. Mental health literacy equips coaches with the skills to detect these subtle changes and intervene early—whether through empathetic conversations, adjustments to training plans, or referrals to mental health professionals.

### Moving beyond crisis management

Traditionally, mental health in sports has often been addressed reactively—only when an athlete is visibly struggling. Mental health literacy shifts this focus from reactive crisis management to proactive care and prevention. Coaches, parents, and others in the support system, with this knowledge, can create environments that reduce the likelihood of mental health struggles in the first place by emphasizing resilience, emotional regulation, and psychological safety.

### Practical applications in grassroots settings

In grassroots sports academies, mental health literacy can manifest in several practical ways:

1. **Recognizing red flags**: Coaches and support staff should be trained to identify warning signs such as changes in behaviour, withdrawal from teammates, irritability, or significant shifts in performance. These signs often precede more serious issues and can be addressed early with proper intervention.
2. **Using everyday language**: Mental health literacy includes the ability to discuss emotions and psychological concepts in a way that resonates with young athletes. For example, instead of using clinical terms like "anxiety," coaches might talk about "feeling nervous" or "pressure moments," making the conversation more relatable.

3. **Promoting Self-Awareness in Athletes**: Athletes can be taught to understand and articulate their emotional states, helping them take ownership of their mental well-being. This could involve journaling exercises, mindfulness activities, or group discussions about handling challenges.

### The role of programs like Project CARE

Programs like INSPA's Project CARE (Cultivating Athlete Resilience through Empowerment) are pivotal in equipping coaches and support staff with the tools and training to foster mental health literacy. CARE emphasizes practical, hands-on learning, teaching participants how to:

- Recognize early signs of mental health challenges.
- Support athletes in building resilience through structured interventions.
- Engage in open conversations about mental health without stigma.
- Integrate mental health practices into regular training routines.

For instance, a CARE-trained coach might begin a practice session with a brief mindfulness exercise to help athletes focus, followed by a team discussion about handling setbacks in competition. These seemingly small practices, when consistently applied, create a culture that normalizes mental well-being as part of athletic development.

### Bridging the gap between Mental Health and Performance

Mental health literacy also addresses a critical misconception in sports—that mental health and performance are separate domains. On the contrary, mental well-being is deeply interconnected with athletic performance. Athletes who are emotionally balanced and mentally resilient are more likely to perform consistently under pressure, recover quickly from failures, and sustain motivation over time.

**For example:**

- An athlete with good mental health literacy might recognize pre-competition nerves as a natural response and use strategies like deep breathing or visualization to manage them.
- A coach who understands this process can reinforce the athlete's confidence by normalizing those feelings and guiding them toward productive coping mechanisms.

### The ripple effect

Finally, mental health literacy is not just about individual athletes—it has a ripple effect on the entire ecosystem of an academy. Coaches with strong mental health awareness model emotionally intelligent behaviour, which influences how athletes interact with each other and their environment. This creates a supportive community where vulnerability is seen as strength, learning is prioritized, and well-being is integral to success.

By embedding mental health literacy into the fabric of grassroots sports academies, we move closer to a culture where young athletes can flourish, not just as performers but as individuals equipped to navigate the challenges of life both on and off the field.

## 2. Creating a Culture of Psychological Safety in Grassroots Sports

Psychological safety is a cornerstone for the resilience, growth, and performance of athletes, particularly at the grassroots level. Drawing from Amy Edmondson's work on psychological safety in organisations, it becomes evident that safe environments are not merely about technical excellence but about cultivating trust, openness, and respect. This is essential for interactions among coaches, peers, and parents, where the athlete's emotional and mental well-being must take precedence.

Parental Involvement and Psychological Safety in the Indian Context

In India, parental involvement is often pivotal in shaping an athlete's journey, but it comes with unique cultural nuances. Traditionally, Indian families emphasize collective aspirations, positioning parents as central decision-makers in their children's sports careers. While this dynamic can provide a robust support system, it may also inadvertently compromise psychological safety. For instance, the high expectations placed on young athletes may discourage them from sharing vulnerabilities, fearing disappointment or criticism.

As the understanding of psychological safety gains traction in Indian sports, shifts are occurring in these traditional dynamics. Increasing awareness through workshops and collaborative efforts between psychologists, coaches, and academies is educating parents about creating emotionally safe environments. These interventions emphasize empathy, open communication, and focusing on effort rather than outcomes.

Camilla Knight's work on parental involvement underscores this shift. Knight advocates for a process-driven approach where parents celebrate effort, learning, and resilience instead of placing undue importance on medals or rankings. For example, at a tennis academy in South India, workshops for parents have encouraged statements like *"Focus on giving your best effort"* over *"You must win."* Such shifts foster autonomy and reduce performance pressure, nurturing an environment where athletes feel supported rather than scrutinized.

Changing perspectives in India illustrate how psychological safety is evolving. Parents are increasingly recognizing the need to balance their support with autonomy. For instance, in a grassroots cricket academy in Western India, parents participated in role-playing exercises during workshops, learning to provide feedback that encouraged rather than criticized. These initiatives align with

Gould and Carson's (2008) emphasis on parental involvement that strengthens bonds and emotional security.

However, cultural and societal pressures persist. In many cases, parents equate their child's success with family honour, inadvertently amplifying performance anxiety. Addressing these challenges requires ongoing education and a collaborative approach to transform these entrenched attitudes.

## Teachers as Key Stakeholders in the Inner Circle

Teachers in residential sports schools face significant pressure to balance academic priorities with the demands of athletic development. This stems from deeply rooted cultural norms in India that historically prioritize academics over sports. Many families and communities regard academic achievement as the primary path to a stable future, with sports seen as secondary or risky.

Consequently, teachers may experience conflicting expectations—to uphold academic rigor while accommodating the needs of student-athletes.

However, in schools where sports dominate, the inverse challenge exists: teachers might feel sidelined as academics take a backseat to athletic pursuits. This creates a tension-filled environment where they must advocate for educational importance while supporting the school's sports-focused ethos.

Shifting Perspectives and Resistance to Change Despite a growing acknowledgment of the importance of balancing academics and sports, full acceptance is not yet widespread. There is resistance to redefining success as a combination of intellectual and athletic excellence.

Many teachers feel unsupported in adapting their roles to align with these evolving dynamics. This hesitance often stems from inadequate training in understanding sports psychology or a lack of institutional frameworks that integrate academic and sports cultures seamlessly.

For instance, teachers may struggle to appreciate how their teaching can complement sports training. As vital members of the inner circle, their mindset and approach significantly affect student-athletes. Whether they encourage critical thinking or help manage academic stress, their contributions can influence the athlete's ability to focus on training and competitions.

Teachers' Role within the Psychologically Aware Inner Circle Just like coaches, parents, support staff, and management, teachers are crucial in creating a psychologically safe environment. They form a bridge between academic and athletic priorities and have the power to shape how student-athletes perceive and balance these aspects of their lives. Teachers often interact with students more frequently than any other stakeholder, giving them unique opportunities to observe, guide, and influence.

**Steps to Mould Teachers into the Inner Circle:**

1. **Training in Sports Psychology**
   Equipping teachers with basic sports psychology knowledge can help them better understand the unique pressures faced by student-athletes. For instance, workshops on recognizing signs of burnout or performance anxiety would enable early interventions.
2. **Fostering Open Communication**
   Teachers should feel comfortable discussing academic challenges with coaches, management, and even parents, creating a cohesive support system for student-athletes.
3. **Encouraging a Growth Mindset**
   Teachers can model and promote a mindset that values effort and learning over fixed notions of success. They can emphasize

transferable skills like discipline and time management, which are essential in both academics and sports.

4. **Collaborative Problem-Solving**
   Initiatives that bring teachers into decision-making processes related to sports schedules and academic demands can reduce the feeling of being overwhelmed or sidelined.
5. **Resilience-Building Exercises**
   Teachers can incorporate resilience-building into their academic sessions, mirroring techniques used in sports training. This might involve stress management activities, encouraging reflection through journaling, or integrating themes of adaptability into the curriculum.

## The Need for Systemic Change

For teachers to truly embrace their role in the inner circle, systemic changes must support this integration. Schools must establish frameworks that explicitly define the relationship between academics and sports. Initiatives like periodic teacher-coach meetings, cross-disciplinary development programs, and recognition of teachers' contributions to athletic successes can create a culture of collaboration and mutual respect.

## Moving Forward

In moulding teachers into the inner circle, the focus must shift from seeing academics and sports as competing priorities to recognizing their complementary roles. When teachers are empowered as partners in an athlete's journey, they can contribute to environments that foster both academic and athletic excellence. By investing in their training and creating supportive systems, schools can ensure that teachers become advocates for the holistic development of student-athletes, balancing the pressures of tradition with the demands of progress.

The inner circle of an athlete—comprising coaches, parents, support staff, management, and teachers in residential sports schools, play a vital role in shaping their journey. These individuals significantly influence athletes, not only by supporting their physical performance but also by fostering mental resilience, emotional balance, and overall well-being. However, each member of this circle faces unique pressures, whether it's parents grappling with expectations, coaches coping with the pressures of perfectionism, or teachers navigating the balance between academics and sports.

To ensure a supportive environment, the inner circle must be intentionally moulded. This involves equipping them with tools like sports psychology training, fostering open communication, and creating systemic frameworks that integrate academics, sports, and mental health. Recognizing and addressing cultural biases—whether prioritizing academics over sports or vice versa—is critical to building a balanced, athlete-centred ecosystem.

When the inner circle collaborates effectively, it creates a safe and nurturing space where athletes can thrive. This unified approach not only enhances athletic performance but also nurtures well-rounded individuals, ready to excel both on and off the field. By investing in the inner circle, we pave the way for sustainable success across the sporting ecosystem.

**Reflection questions**

The inner circle—parents, coaches, teachers, and support staff—plays a pivotal role in shaping an athlete's journey. Their influence extends beyond technical training or academic support, impacting the athlete's mindset, emotional resilience, and overall well-being.

**Reflective Questions with Context For Parents:**

Parents often balance hopes for their child's success with the need to ensure their mental and physical health. Misaligned expectations or overemphasis on winning can hinder growth.

1. How do I express my support after both successes and failures?
2. Do I engage in open conversations about their goals and challenges?
3. How am I fostering independence and resilience in my child?

**For Coaches:**

Coaches are often the athlete's closest mentors, shaping skills, confidence, and discipline. The challenge lies in balancing high performance with holistic development.

1. Am I emphasizing intrinsic motivation over external rewards?
2. How do I handle moments of conflict between pushing for results and prioritizing the athlete's well-being?
3. What strategies do I use to ensure constructive feedback doesn't harm the athlete's self-esteem?

**For Teachers in Residential Sports Schools:**

Teachers are integral in bridging academics and sports, but societal pressures often skew priorities. The shift towards holistic education is slow and requires advocacy.

1. How can I make learning engaging for athletes, balancing sport and academics?
2. Am I creating a safe space where athletes feel understood and valued for more than just performance?
3. How do I address the tension between societal expectations for academic excellence and the athlete's sports focus?

**For Management and Support Staff:**

Management decisions set the tone for an athlete's environment. Pressure for immediate results or rigid structures may overshadow support for long-term growth.

1. How do my policies reflect a commitment to athlete-centric values?
2. Are we investing in mental health and life skills training for athletes?
3. How am I ensuring alignment and collaboration among all stakeholders in the athlete's ecosystem?

**Cross-Cutting Questions:**

Every member of the inner circle impacts the athlete's journey, whether directly or indirectly. Collaboration and alignment are crucial.

1. Am I actively seeking feedback from the athlete to improve my role?
2. How do I ensure my personal biases don't inadvertently influence their decisions?
3. What steps am I taking to educate myself about mental and emotional well-being to better support them?

# SUSTAINABLE HIGH-PERFORMANCE CULTURES IN SPORT -

MUDIT KRISHNANI

## Introduction

I remember getting my first football jersey. It was the iconic Arsenal home shirt, red and white and ever so glorious. Something on the back side of the badge caught the eye of 14-year-old me - A Latin phrase, embroidered in a bold font, which would make me fall in love with the club even more. “Victoria Concordia Crescit”. “Victory lies in Harmony”. Arsenal’s motto. Even at that young age, that motto made me realize that there is much more to Arsenal than 11 people playing football every week for 90 minutes.

When he was the manager of Liverpool, Jurgen Klopp mentioned in an interview, “My dream was always that we could play in any random shirt… but if you watch us play, you would say ‘Ah, that’s Liverpool’.” (1)

These examples indicate how a team is much more than a collection of individuals who get together, train, and compete in a sport. The “much more” element that separates one team from a set of individuals is what culture is all about.

*The values, the rules, and the environment that guide beliefs and behaviours of the team or organisation.*

While there have been different understandings and definitions of organisational culture over time (2), I've found that the aforementioned

*Activity: Let's take a deep dive into how culture manifests itself with a quick activity. Imagine that you are a player at a residential youth academy of a prestigious cricket club.*

*Situation 1:*
*Your training is fully and only focused on the technical and tactical aspects. Sometimes, when your head coach is unavailable, the assistant coach leads the training sessions, and his drills and approach are totally different from the head coach. Your hostel walls are plain except for a pin board where the coach puts up the team list on game nights. The best players were almost always guaranteed to start, and the coach focuses on the development of specifically those players. There are certain disciplinary regulations to help maintain the "image" of the club, related to dress codes, curfews and interactions with the opposite sex etc.*

*Situation 2:*
*Coaches explicitly talk about the club's vision often and design training sessions in line with the long-term goals of the club.Regardless of whether the head coach or the assistant coach is leading, the sessions maintain a similar objective and approach. The hostel walls are adorned with a lot of photo and paintings displaying the senior team's latest accolades, the academy teams' recent achievements, and the club's values and vision. Coaches communicate team selection during face-to-face meetings. They offer individual feedback and communicate reasons to players who are rested for the game. The focus is on the collective development of each player on the team. The regulations revolve around the club values of respect and honesty, such as wearing proper kit, greeting coaches/staff, keeping shoes clean etc.*

*What are some clear and some subtle differences between the two situations? Reflect on the values, the rules and the environment.*

explanation captures the essence and provides a comprehensive yet very practical perspective.

We can sum up all the differences between these two situations with one word: Culture.

| Difference | Situation 1 | Situation 2 |
|---|---|---|
| Values | Focus on star players | Focus on collective development |
| Rules | Discipline focused | Respect focused |
| Environm ent | No visible artefacts; focus only on sport training; dissonance in coaching approach | Visible artefacts of the club's history, present; explicit mentions of club values; consonance in coaching approach. |

Now, there is no one way of achieving performance excellence. Across time and sports, successful coaches/teams have had different philosophies (think Jose Mourinho's Chelsea vs Pep Guardiola's Manchester City), players who failed to perform with one team have had immense success with another team (think Shane Watson with RCB vs Shane Watson with CSK).

Culture has the ability to provide synergistic values, a shared vision, a collective identity, a purpose, and align expectations from each member. This is what enables a group of performers to come together and perform at a high level, consistently, both as a team and as individuals.

Sometimes, players and coaches may not align on the culture. Dissonant values, different expectations, etc., may hamper performances of even the best players. For example, soon after Pep Guardiola joined Barcelona, Ronaldinho and Deco, two all-time greats of football, left the team. According to their teammate Alexander Hleb, the reason was mostly culture-related (3) – the new coach demanded more professionalism and commitment on and off the field, and they didn't fit in: Pep was afraid they would drag the others down.

They were still great players, but they were not the right fit for the new system. Ronaldinho and Barcelona were both going through a rough performance patch in 2008, but after he left, Barcelona won the treble that very year, and Ronaldinho, although struggling to find his form for a bit, shone through in the next season for his new club.

Culture, and being the right fit, as you can then see, is an important factor in unlocking performance excellence. Hence, if one can establish an effective culture, high performance will take care of itself.

Why this chapter? How did you get into this area of work?

During the early stages of my career as a sport psychology practitioner, I was working with an elite youth football academy. As an eager practitioner, I had dived right into understanding the needs of each athlete. I would spend most of my time immersed in individual sessions, building tailored interventions to boost performance, develop psychosocial skills, and maintain mental health across all age groups. It was effective, at least on the surface. I saw the boys grow, stay committed to their goals, feel more confident, and so on.

However, there was a moment when my conviction in that approach came crashing down. A U-16 player came for a session and burst into tears. He left the club a week after that. He told me he "hates" the new team's coach. A lot of what he told me about the coach's behaviour was something that I was aware of, but there was one eye-opening statement for me. He told me how it was hard to climb up the ranks and play for the senior team because the coaches are so different. One year, your coach tells you to focus on developing your skills and encourages making mistakes, and the next year you are immediately taken off the team/benched after a mistake–with no feedback except for a good shout at. He mentioned how the senior team players play with a totally different approach than the U-18s and U-16 s.

Now, tactics and techniques are not the expertise of a sport psychologist, but he had a solid point. Essentially, if the younger age groups are playing differently, being coached differently, without any communication/structure– they are being set up to fail. Once they reach the next level, almost all of what they have learnt and the way they have learnt is thrown out the window, and they must adapt to their new coach's style. If they fail to do so, the onus is on them, and they are substituted, benched, and eventually released.

I realized at that point that I had been oblivious to a key element of consistent high performance: culture.

The reason I write this chapter is to guide neophyte practitioners, athletes, parents, coaches, and sport enthusiasts about this very important element of consistent high performance. Instinctively, as well as guided by the thought process of "controlling the controllables," it is often easy to misunderstand "culture" as an uncontrollable. Hence, when we, or our athletes, or our children, face a situation where the environment is not suitable for growth, we tend to look inwards. "You must adapt", "You must adjust", "Trust the coach", "You can't always have things your way".

While I agree with the importance of being adaptable and flexible, the athlete alone is not fully responsible for consistent high performance. The environment plays a huge role – what the athlete hears from her team, coaches, family, what the athlete sees in the dressing room, the unspoken rules, the bonding with her teammates, the knowledge (or lack thereof) of the purpose of her endeavours… all of this, and much more, forms her culture, and guides performance.

And yes, cultures can be identified, built, and modified.

The chapter

Studies suggest that the culture of a team or organisation plays a vital role in the success of an organisation (2). Specifically in sport, culture has been suggested to contribute to the cohesion and performance of teams (4–7).

If we dig deeper into the mechanisms of how culture works, you might think it's pretty evident and straightforward: What we see and hear around us affects how we perceive things, and hence how we behave.

In an ideal world, that would be exactly how it works. But in the real world, it gets messy. What we see, feel, and hear around us might differ between training and home, day to day, within the academy/ training centre, between coaches, management, and support staff…

and so on. Often, there is conscious or unconscious dissonance between the words and actions of people. Sometimes, we might feel we have "built" a culture without realizing that it is a dynamic process and only effective if it is consistently reinforced.

For example, in a workshop with team sport coaches and support staff, I asked them what the values of their organisation are. I was hoping they'd quickly identify these, especially since they're written right on the wall of their office. Unfortunately, as a group, they could only remember 3 out of 5. After digging into this a bit and trying to understand how a group of 30 people was unable to recall the values that are visible to them every single day, I realized that the values were not being reinforced. In daily, weekly and monthly team discussions, the discussions were about things similar to the values, but other words would be used by the management without any reference to the organisational values. In individual annual reviews, there was no part that assessed the staff on these values. There were no discussions about the application of these values - how they operate on the pitch, or the hierarchy. Hence, there is a need to build and consciously reinforce culture: It is important to incorporate a very comprehensive understanding of the term and understand the dynamicity of the process.

Let's talk about building a culture, then. There are multiple theoretical models of high-performance culture across sport and organisational psychology (e.g. 8–10), and the one I chose to adapt is by Jake Humphrey and Damian Hughes (11). I lean towards this particular model because it's comprehensive, dynamic, and is easy to explain to stakeholders.

Jake and Damian take from a series of studies done in the 1990s by James Baron and Michael Hannan on organisational culture in the Silicon Valley and highlight a *commitment-focused culture* as an effective, sustainable high-performance culture among the 5 identified blueprints of organisational culture (12).

> *Activity: Think about an organisation/team that you are working with or have worked with. Reflect on the following:*
>
> *Values – what are the values? Are they visible? How often are they reinforced? How is value-guided behaviour rewarded?*
>
> *People – what motivates most of them to show up? What is the basis of selection for new people? What kind of behaviour is rewarded?*
>
> *Goals – what is the priority of the organisation/team? How often are shared goals reinforced? How consonant are the priorities and goals with the values?*

**A commitment culture has the following features:**

- People work with the organisation primarily because of a strong connection with the purpose and teammates/colleagues.
- "People" are at the heart of this culture. Organisations/leaders listen to the people and make decisions with the interest of the people as a priority.
- Onboarding or selection is done primarily based on how well the people fit into the values and vision.

To build a commitment culture, there are three elements to work on (11), as shown in figure 1.

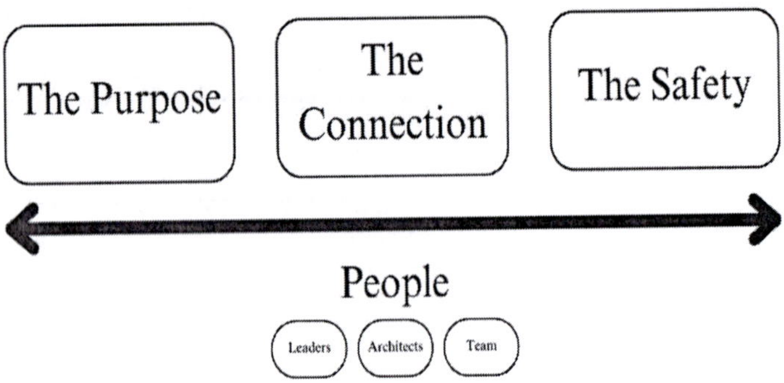


**Figure 1: Components of a commitment culture. Self-made, based on (11).**

## The purpose

This is what glues the organisation or team together. In a commitment culture, purpose plays a huge role in getting the right people and motivating them to continue to work. Depending on the organisation's vision, they have different mission statements. Consider the following examples:

Walt Disney: To make people happy (original)/We make happy happen (current)

Coca-Cola: Refresh the world. Make a difference. Pfizer: Working together for a healthier world.

Nike: To bring inspiration and innovation to every athlete in the world. Arsenal FC: To act for a winning team, culture, and community.

FC Bayern Munich: To inspire with outstanding experiences - and with the essence of what makes us successful.

Each of these statements gives an insight into what the specific organisation or team considers important and what motivates them to continue working hard. It indicates the values of the organisation as well.

For example, for Arsenal Football Club–community and togetherness stand out as big values based on their mission statement, which has also translated to actions: During the COVID-19 lockdown, Arsenal continued to pay their staff and launched community initiatives to support those affected by the pandemic. To make up for the losses, they became the first Premier League club to ask players to take a pay cut – the players agreed, as did the manager (13).

The idea here is to not just build or discover a mission statement and let it be, but to actually reinforce the purpose and shared values. This gives people a chance to connect with a bigger picture that goes beyond just sustenance or livelihood and motivates them in a way similar to what Abraham Maslow described as self-actualisation. Hence, mission statements and values go hand in hand as part of the purpose.

Hence, building the purpose is a two-step process:

**Step 1: Finding the "why." It's a simple but vital question to think about:** "Why are we doing this?" Humphrey and Hughes (11) suggest a Socratic questioning manner, prodding to figure out the root "why". An example of this is a conversation I had with the head coach of a football team:

> *MK: Coach, why are we training so hard and pushing ourselves so much?*
>
> *Coach: To be the best we can be. MK: Why do we want to be the best?*
>
> *Coach: To win promotion (to the next league), MK: Why do we want to win promotion?*
>
> *Coach: To show that we belong in the top division.*
>
> *MK: Why do we want to show that we belong in the top division? Coach: To show that a team from a small town is capable of greatness. MK: Why do we want to show that?*
>
> *Coach: To inspire every kid who does not have access to a lot of resources and show that they can also achieve their dreams.*

There you have your purpose. The big "why". Why are we playing for this team?

*To empower and inspire every young person, regardless of resources, to believe in their potential and pursue their dreams.*

How does reading that mission statement make you feel? Compare it to how the statement "To be the best we can be" makes you feel, and you'll immediately notice the difference, and hence the importance of this kind of prodding.

In all fairness, the conversation did not go exactly as I've described – there was a bit of frustration expressed by the coach because of the incessant whys, but it helped identify the purpose and motivation that was the foundation for a commitment culture.

*Activity: Speak to a coach/technical director and try to find their team's "why" using this technique. Reflect on what went well and what the blockers were.*

**Step 2: Reinforcing the "why":** Now that we've found our why, let's ensure visibility and retention.

It's common for teams to put up the purpose statement, values, operating principles, or commandments on a wall, give one seminar about the vision, and believe their task is complete. That is a key component to increase visibility, but unfortunately, that alone does not work.

Going back to that workshop where the staff couldn't recall the organisation's values, even though they saw them every day at the office – That is a prime example of how a lot of organisations view this element. However, every bit of culture is dynamic. Yes, your values and purpose might remain the same across time and situations... but unless they are reinforced, repeated and given importance in assessments, they will be forgotten. The staff and athletes are too busy planning sessions, game plans, and tactics, due to which they're already stretched for time, on top of which they face tons of personal and organisational stressors. Which brings the question of "what reason will they even have to care about some words that are written on a board in front of their desk or the changing room?

To get the team to integrate the values and shared purpose into their individual approaches, there are two key strategies: Reason and Reiteration. There needs to be a reason for them to care –

1. It can be organic: Linking the purpose with individual goals, values to build common goals. For example, the purpose of empowering kids can be linked to the outcome goal of winning promotion, and then into daily, actionable process goals.
2. It can be induced: For example, integrating values/purpose statement within performance reviews/appraisals (via commandments/operating principles* etc.), or having a peer recognition system based on the values (player of the month based on value-related behaviour as well as performance etc.)

**Commandments/operating principles here refer to pre-defined value-driven behaviours*

Reiteration is then almost a by-product, where leaders are overtly using the shared purpose in their strategies, sessions, and reports, hence reinforcing them at regular intervals.

Let's see how this works. Imagine you're coaching a youth basketball team. The purpose statement is "To build a basketball community where players lift each other up, develop a deep respect for teammates and opponents, and strive to set new standards of skill." The academy, hence has "unity" as a huge value and has a commandment: "We make sure our actions are helping our team perform better." Everyone has been told that they will not only be assessed on their league position/results, but also on the commandments, because they are an important element of being at the academy. You are then likely to use the operating principles consciously as reference points when planning training sessions, setting goals and expectations for the players.

Hence, you are likely to talk about and build drills that promote unity/team-focused decision making.

**The connection**

Think about your best friend(s). The person, or people who understand you, can read your emotions and feelings, know how to support you… Hughes talks about a similar connection where a team or group has a bond based on mutual respect and emotional sensitivity.

I once had a young athlete come up and talk to me about the sudden death of a parent. Understandably, he was devastated… but the way the club handled it was amazing to see. The club planned for not only him, but his coaches and teammates as well to attend the last rites and show their respect. The organisation and team were there for him, strengthening the emotional bond – communicating to him (and the rest of the team), via actions, that they will be there for each other through thick and thin.

In a similar example, take the armed forces. They are the most elite high-performance team, literally facing life-or-death situations daily. "No man left behind" is a popular phrase associated with armed forces across movies, books, and songs, which clearly highlights the importance of having a connection and knowing your team has your back.

Such a connection makes people stick around for the long term and stay committed to giving their best– for a team that cares.

To build this connection, there are two key skills: Empathy and compassion. Empathy and compassion across management, leaders, and teams.

Empathy and compassion come from emotional quotient. Emotional intelligence training, hence, becomes a very important element of building sustainable high-performance cultures. As a practitioner, interventions revolving around active listening, vulnerability, and effective communication can be utilised – underpinned by building a "person-centric" approach where the team members are viewed as "people who play the sport" first, and "high performers" second. Because when you start looking at athletes or colleagues as individuals, you begin to understand and value their emotions, their vulnerabilities, their sacrifices… You begin to care about them… you start to build a connection with them.

On a daily level, this manifests as an organic interest in lives beyond sport/job: inquiring about the well-being of the guard, remembering the names of and checking in on the family of the hostel warden, engaging with teammates in other activities like shopping, movies, etc. I've seen bonds where teammates trust each other so much that they cut each other's hair!! When the team knows you have their back on and off the pitch, they will give their best for each other.

**The safety**

No one is perfect. Even the best of the best make all kinds of mistakes: Technical mistakes, emotional mistakes, tactical mistakes. Even though they have bad performances and lose matches or competitions. Think about Lionel Messi – being unable to win a major international trophy after coming very close multiple times, frustrated to the point of announcing retirement…before he came back and was an instrumental element in the Copa America, and eventually the World Cup-winning squads.

So, it's safe to say that players will make mistakes. Lots of them. The key, then, is to learn from them. Be it Rocky Balboa's "It ain't about how hard you hit. It's about how hard you can get hit and keep moving forward" or Batman Begins' "Why do we fall, Bruce? So, we can learn to pick ourselves up" – even movies about high performance seem to get it right: People will make mistakes, and that's okay.

The challenge arises when people don't feel safe enough to make or admit their mistakes. To take risks, to try for that creative pass, that insane dribble… They fear the outcome of failure. A loss. A scolding by the coach. Teammates holding grudges. Getting dropped from the team. Being looked at as incompetent… that makes for an unsafe environment.

Psychological safety refers to perceptions of the consequences of taking interpersonal risks in a particular context (14). In sport, a safe environment makes for an environment where athletes and staff are comfortable being themselves, taking risks and seeking support (15), and has been linked with high-performance (16), team resilience (17), and lower burnout (18), hence being a key part of a sustainable high-performance culture.

Observations, surveys, and interviews are common and reliable ways to understand the existing sense of safety within a team. Reactions of players and coaches after mistakes, risk-taking behaviours on the pitch, how coaches give/receive feedback, pre-game talks, post-game debriefs, the awards/rewards system, mechanisms/ways to address personal concerns of athletes… all these point towards how safe/unsafe the culture is.

Going back to that incident about the U-16 player who left the club and made me realise the importance of culture – he went from an encouraging and safe environment (the U-15 team) to an unsafe environment where mistakes were punished by shouting and getting dropped from the team.

*Activity - The psychological safety checklist (Appendix A): Use this checklist to reflect on the psychological safety of a team/organisation you are/were a part of.*

Once the team is aware of their existing behaviours, both helpful and unhelpful, vis-à-vis safety, you can start to reinforce safety-promoting behaviours and reassess the safety at regular intervals (a month, for example).

These include encouraging/constructive reactions to mistakes, pushing players out of their comfort zone, highlighting calculated risk efforts, implementing an effective 360 feedback loop, process-focused talks and reflective debriefs, and effective redressal mechanisms for concerns. This might involve sitting down with the management or coaching staff and defining a "safety net" for the team, which will help set expectations from the players and the coaches.

Making mistakes will always remain a part of sport, but a safe environment is when players are more likely to admit their mistakes and try to improve them, whereas an unsafe environment would lead to hiding of mistakes, and hence less likelihood of improvement.

**The people**

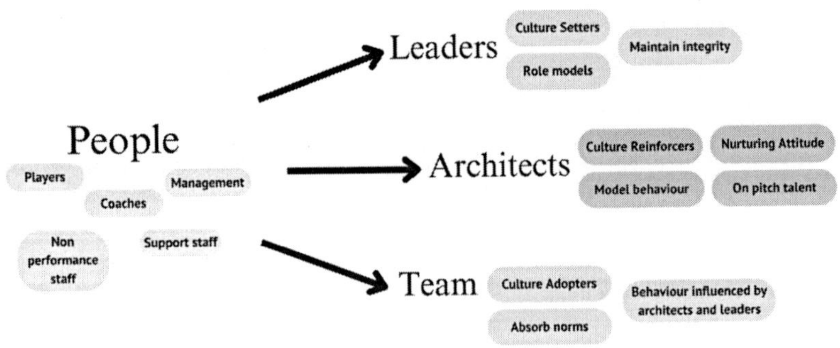


**Figure 2: People of a team culture. Self-made, based on (11).**

The overarching piece that culture is all about: People. In a sports team, these would include everyone from the players to management, coaches, support staff, and non-performance staff as well. Specifically, from a culture cultural point of view, people can largely be viewed as having one of three roles: Leaders, Architects, and "the team". Out of these three, leaders and architects are the ones who can have a major influence on the team's culture.

**Leaders:**

These people are the role models, the "culture setters" as it were. They guide the behaviour of the team by leading via by example. If the team sees the leader lose control and shout at the officials, they will learn that as an acceptable behaviour, and it will soon become a norm. If the team sees the leader excuse themselves from the rules and regulations, the seniors will start making exceptions for certain rules for themselves… and it too will become a norm.

We shall discuss how different leadership styles affect culture but there is one thing that plays a key role in creating a commitment culture: Integrity. Leaders who are accountable, transparent, and fair in their decisions help build that emotional bond and safety.

In India, especially in sports which are politically rife, I've seen multiple situations where disciplinary actions were not taken, or reversed, simply due to favouritism, or political connections. From simple but impactful things like the star player being excused from punishment when they arrive late at training to hushed decisions of politically connected players being forgiven for physical abuse, a lack of integrity in leaders affects the culture. The motivating factors in such a culture revolve around getting into the good books of the leaders, instead of excelling and mastering their skills. This then causes a hyper-competitive environment where there is no safety net for making mistakes, and the team indulges in cut-throat competition, ready to throw each other under the bus at the blink of an eye. Such a culture will limit the performance and hamper the well-being of its people.

So, you may choose to prioritize one leadership style over another, but without integrity, everything will fall apart. Considering integrity to be maintained, let's explore how a few approaches to leadership work to build sustainable, high-performance cultures.

## Servant Leaders:

Think about Phil Jackson. The legendary basketball coach known for his love for "zen" and mindfulness. His approach to leadership revolved around prioritising and empowering the team and their needs. He made sure that he treats every player with the same respect, leading by example. Athletes were offered all the support and guidance while being pushed to take ownership of their own growth. This kind of player focused leadership style is very similar to a servant leadership style (19). The result? A safe environment with trust and integrity being maintained to catalyse growth. This approach led him to 11 NBA championships across two teams, making him the most decorated coach in NBA history.

## Transformational Leaders:

In essence, transformational leadership is about inspiring the people around you to excel and exceed their limits (20). Jurgen Jürgen Klopp, former Dortmund and Liverpool manager, is a great example of such leadership. His very first message when he joined Liverpool? "Turning doubters into believers." (21) This shared vision, combined with his approach where the team is above and beyond individual players, led to an environment with high integrity, a strong emotional bond, and motivation to learn from mistakes. This helped Liverpool to achieve eight major trophies in the nine years he was in charge, including an elusive Champions League title and Liverpool's first league title in 30 years.

**Identity Leadership (22):**

Sir Alex Ferguson is considered one of the all-time greats in football coaching history. He managed Manchester United for 26 years and won a historic 13 league titles. A key part of his approach was instilling a sense of pride in the players: They were playing for the historic Manchester United, they should know the history and values of the club (23). They were expected to uphold the club's traditions, creating a strong, consistent identity across generations. Ferguson would often emphasise this pride and identity during matches with title rivals such as Liverpool and Arsenal: These matches were almost a battle to protect the pride of the club. When leaders create such an identity of "us"

within a team, they strengthen their identity as a team with shared purpose, rather than a group of 11 individuals with separate goals (24).

When building cultures, leaders need to be made aware of the impact of their behaviour and style of leadership. They can choose servant, transformational, identity (or even any other suitable style that promotes creating a shared purpose, emotional bonds, and psychological safety) styles, or even a mix of those! As long as they maintain integrity and the right priorities: Creating a shared vision, promoting emotional bonds and psychological safety while embodying these things themselves will lead to changes in the team culture. One such change could be noticing the presence of cultural architects. Those within the team who embody the purpose actively make connections and ensure safety.

**Architects:**

Coaches and management are the auto-designated, hierarchical culture leaders: They are expected to (for good reason) set the rules, expectations, and lead by example. However, there are others in the team: players who are not expected to set the rules and/or lead by example, but they fit into the culture well, and their actions reinforce the commitment culture. These people are important for a simple reason: Conformity. Hughes quotes Solomon Asch's seminal work on conformity and how the presence of a single voice within the group can change the whole dynamic of the group, and these people, who set the right example, are called cultural architects.

Humphrey and Hughes (11) talk about three things that help identify these architects: model behaviour, nurturing attitude, and on-pitch talent.

1. Model behaviour refers to showing commitment via actions. This could include arriving early to training, behaving professionally on and off the pitch. Tony Adams, who embodied the culture of Arsenal during his time at the club (now aptly called Mr Arsenal) once spoke about the importance of playing for the badge in front of the shirt – I find it interesting to observe how players celebrate: some of them kiss the badge, some of them celebrate with teammates, some will even run a long way to celebrate with the staff… Those are the model behaviours that show commitment to the team. Take Cristiano Ronaldo, for example: He was a key figure in Portugal's 2016 Euro victory, but from a culture perspective, two moments stepped out: During a penalty shootout against Poland, he was seen talking to a teammate, reminding him that he takes good penalties and it's okay if they lose (25). Second, during the final, he was stretchered off the pitch, cameras focused on his tearful eyes. However, soon after that, he was seen on the touchline next to his coach, limping, but eager to support

and rally the team (26). Both instances show how he wanted to support his teammates and help them perform at their best while feeling safe.

2. A nurturing attitude is about wanting to protect and nurture other team members, helping them settle in and feel at home. Rohit Sharma has spoken a lot about how Sachin Tendulkar was such a figure in the Indian men's cricket team dressing room: showing the ropes and being just a call away for support. (27) This support builds the emotional bond and safety that is required for players to excel consistently, through the ups and downs of high performance.
3. On-pitch talent helps command the attention and respect of fellow teammates. It helps them see the connection between model behaviour, nurturing attitude, and high performance. That these behaviours are not just for the sake of rules or because they're "kind" people: It's for consistent high performance at the top level.

Find these architects and empower them. Involve them in decision making processes (if possible), highlight their behaviour, show the team you care about these... and it will create a ripple effect where motivating people to embody the behaviours of the architects, fostering leadership throughout the team to support the coaches and pass down the culture from one group to another.

When finding architects, it could also be someone who may not be currently on the team but does display all three elements. I was working with a club that really valued their youth academy and had a long-term plan of building a homegrown team, inspired by Alex Ferguson's class of 92. When repainting the academy recreation room, they made a mural of the senior team in a huddle: No one's face was visible, but two jerseys were. They could've chosen the star striker or the new international signee, both bought recently by the club for huge money, both inspirational names in the sport.

However, they put the names and numbers of two youngsters on the jerseys. Two youngsters who were great role models, hard workers, and exceptionally skilled. Two youngsters who had made it from the academy: Two cultural architects.

Building a shared purpose, emotional bonds, and a safe environment will help create a culture that has the potential to help people commit to giving their best and excel in a sustainable way. The potential can be converted into reality by having the right people, who buy into the purpose and embody the behaviours to lead by example.

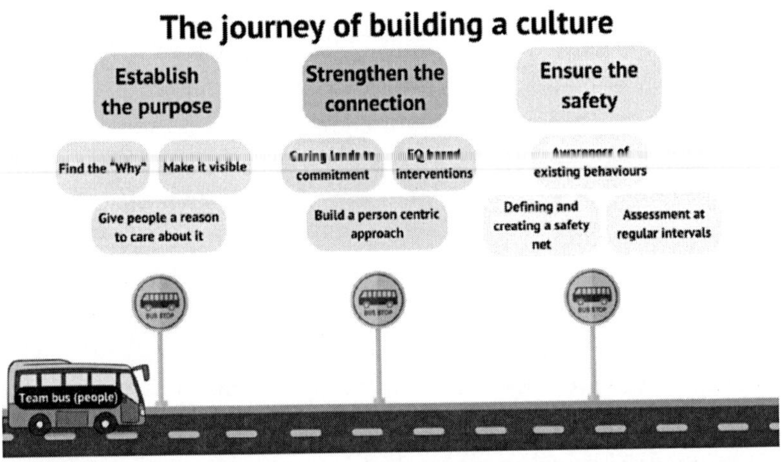


**Figure 3: The journey of building a culture. Like a bus route, the journey is a constant process of reiteration and repetition of the same stops again and again. Self-made.**

*Activity – Think about a team/organisation you are working/ have worked with.*

*Reflect on the leaders:*

*Who came to your mind and what made you think of them? (Behaviours, role hierarchy in team etc.)*

*Reflect on some of the leader behaviours that were adopted by the team members as norms*

*Try and identify some cultural architects:*

*Reflect on what makes each of them an architect? (Model behaviour, nurturing attitude, or on pitch talent)*

*Reflect on how/if the architects are appreciated/honoured.*

*Identify three key factors that are currently helping build a strong commitment culture within the organisation.*

*Think about three changes you would implement to enhance sustainable high performance within the organisation.*

## Challenges

People are integral to a culture – hence the importance of having the right people. Not only in terms of skill or talent, but in terms of the right culture fit. This becomes incredibly challenging when hiring decisions are made without considering cultural fit. Think about how each coach prefers different players, regardless of skill. Sunil Chhetri (28) once spoke about how, around the beginning of his career, he was on the bench for his team when the striker got injured. He was preparing to replace him and get his opportunity to shine, but the coach asked the injured striker to continue playing. Later, Sunil mentions hearing the coach apologize to the striker for not being able to substitute him because of a lack of strikers on the bench… This had nothing to do with the skill of Sunil Chhetri, who is now the highest goal scorer for India and in the ISL, but perhaps something to do with the coach's vision and idea for the team.

Imagine you were the psychologist in that club. Admittedly, the coach would have handled the situation differently, with more empathy towards the young striker on the bench. At the same time, the crux of the situation is that no one is inherently wrong. A coach will always want players who fit into their system, follow their rules… players who they can trust.

On the other hand, each player has a unique skill set, mindset, and approach to sport that may not always align with the coach or team. When working with culture, you will find people who are not the right fit with the culture/vision of the organisation/team. The challenge here is multifold:

Should you attempt to align the personal values of those who don't fit with the shared values and their individual goals with the common goals?

Is it your place to determine whether certain players or staff will struggle to succeed within the culture?

In a lot of instances, livelihood is a big motivator for people to continue working in an organisation/team setup even if they know it's not the right fit. Especially in India, where a lot of people put the needs of their family before their own, and organised employment in the sports sector is not very promising... people might agree to change their behaviour to keep their place in the team or a job as support staff. Sometimes, they will change their behaviour and buy into the purpose, but sometimes their words will fail to convert into action.

At the end of the day, it is important to reflect on our priorities and role. As a sport psychology practitioner, your role in most circumstances will not include human resources. Being assessed on culture fit might be an important element of an organisation's performance reviews, but your role is to support people to accept and align themselves with the culture to reach professional and personal goals. When we talk about building a culture with safety, we prioritise creating an environment where athletes and staff feel safe and comfortable enough to acknowledge and work on certain areas of improvement, while providing them with all the tools necessary to overcome their current barriers. That is, in my experience, the most effective strategy to navigate this challenge while staying true to your role.

Another common challenge I've faced revolves around different stakeholders having different values or understanding of values. Respect is one great example of this in the Indian context. I've met a lot of coaches who believe the athletes they coach are expected to agree with what they are saying, talking back is considered disrespectful. I was working with one such coach, and the organisation had a clearly defined operating principle for "Respect."

***"In our team, respect means valuing each other's voices, competing fairly, supporting one another, and consistently striving to improve ourselves. We show respect through giving and accepting constructive feedback, inclusive communication, and fairness in our actions."***

This clearly indicates that the organisation is looking for those who value everyone's opinions and feedback. This was reiterated and reinforced multiple times by the management. Yet the coach would indicate that players are not showing respect based on his own understanding–if they didn't touch his feet, if they gave some feedback/suggestion to him, etc. And this is one of many such instances I have faced, across values such as unity, integrity, trust, and so on

In such situations, a suitable strategy is to sit down and have some overt, targeted conversations. It's messy, it's uncomfortable, but it can be very insightful. A lot of the conversation will be guided by the rapport that you have with the coach/staff/athlete, but a useful template to go on would be this:

| Objective | Example |
|---|---|
| Acknowledging a shared goal | "Hi, coach, thanks for agreeing to this chat. I know we're both focused on helping the athletes grow, so I wanted to discuss something important that can help us align even more." |
| Introducing purpose/ topic | "I've noticed some differences in how 'respect' is interpreted by different members of the team. Since it's a core value in our organisation, I thought it might be helpful to clarify and explore how we all view and apply it in practice." |
| Sharing observations without judgement | "For instance, I've seen that respect in our organisation includes open communication, where everyone's voice can be heard. However, I've also noticed that sometimes players hesitate to share feedback or ideas with you. It could be because they want to respect your position, but it's affecting the open communication we aim for." |
| Inviting their perspective | "How do you see respect in a coaching context? Are there certain behaviours from athletes that you feel are respectful or disrespectful? I'd like to understand your perspective on this." |
| Clarifying organisational definition | "Thanks for sharing that. From the organisation's point of view, respect also means being able to listen to each other's feedback constructively and engaging in open conversations. We encourage athletes to share thoughts because it helps us all improve." |

| | |
|---|---|
| Offering a segue and agreeing on action | "I understand that the athletes sharing suggestions might feel different from what you're used to. Maybe we could find a way for them to give feedback that maintains a tone you're comfortable with while still upholding this open communication principle - What if we set specific team meetings for this purpose, where athletes can share feedback? That way, we're all on the same page about when and how this dialogue happens." |
| Assuring commitment and concluding | "Does this approach feel workable to you? I think it could create a strong foundation for how we bring 'respect' to life in the team. Thanks for taking the time to talk about this with me. I really value how committed you are to making the team the best it can be." |

These conversations will often go differently than you'd expect, so the key here is to remember your objectives and guide conversations back to them if they start to digress, while being non-judgemental and listening actively.

Building or modifying organisational culture is a non-linear process. You will face challenges, roadblocks. You will feel like you're taking two steps forward, one step back. You will feel like banging your head against the wall… but at the end of that tunnel, there is a light. There is a realisation that slowly, but surely, you're creating an impact. Weak signs of the common purpose being reinforced here and there in coach speeches. Architects of a commitment culture are starting to become evident and empowering others around them to do the same. A small safety net for the team… then a bigger safety net… and so on.

## Reflections

I want to share some key experiences here that might be worth exploring while evaluating the effectiveness of building cultures.

Sustainability is a key ingredient in high-performance cultures: Environments that seem well suited for high-performance might end up suffering from turnover and burnout concerns if sustainability is missing.

Being able to perform at the highest level *consistently* is then arguably the most important element to succeed in the long run. Hence, the term "sustainable high-performance cultures". Sustainability is the backbone of culture, and here are a few reflections to help you identify how sustainable the high-performance culture is:

a. Signs of sustainability of the culture you are creating –
b. Is there a reason for people to care about values and purpose?
c. How exactly is "culture fit" being integrated into the onboarding process?
d. How are new team members being made aware of the shared purpose and common goals?
e. How is the human side of performers being actively prioritised?
f. How do people treat those "lower" than themselves in the traditional hierarchy, especially when no one's looking? In terms of showing respect (remembering names, shaking hands, listening to them, and caring about their lives, etc.)
g. How big is the safety net? Is it acceptable to make 1 mistake, 10 mistakes, or 100 mistakes? Is it acceptable to make mistakes in training but not in competition?

How is the balance between achieving results/high-performance and athlete well-being & burnout being maintained and evaluated?

1. Here's what has helped me:
2. Including culture fit as part of the onboarding process is a good way to try and replace people with others who fit into the culture. Sometimes, you may not be able to influence or implement that, and that's okay. Another strategy is to document the culture and create cultural artefacts across the team/organisation.
3. If culture is informal and unwritten, it's easier for a new person to influence it, whereas to remove and replace already existing posters, photos, wall paintings, assessment practices, etc., requires more effort.

You can also try to link the culture to values that go beyond just one team/leader – upper management, assistant coaches, senior players, or even at an organisational level.

## Conclusion

To build and sustain high-performance cultures, a commitment-focused culture is key, where people are motivated to perform for a strong connection with the shared purpose. This is achieved by the organisation keeping people at its core interest and having culture fit as a key element of onboarding new staff and players.

There are three key elements that make up a commitment culture: Purpose, Connection, and Safety. Leaders and cultural architects are major drivers of culture through their rules and actions. When people see leaders behave in certain ways, it sets the norm for the team.

To find the purpose, discuss the core values of the organisation, and try to find an answer to the question "Why are we doing this?" Keep digging till you get to the core reason. Make sure this purpose aligns with team and individual goals, and is reinforced heavily in reviews, talks, discussions, and decision-making.

Emotional bonds are an important part of building connections. Coupled with interventions around active listening and vulnerability, a people-centric approach where people are individuals first and athletes/staff second will ensure the team has a strong bond on and off the pitch.

Psychological safety allows people to be themselves and admit mistakes. As a result, they are more likely to take calculated risks and put effort into improving their mistakes. Identifying existing behaviours regarding safety and then developing an approach that promotes safety on and off the pitch is key.

Reaction to mistakes, post-game debriefs, and pre-game talks are some important areas to observe and modify, if necessary.

Leadership is key to bringing all this together. If they are unwilling to find the purpose, to create an empathic, compassionate team and lead by integrity and example, the culture will head in an unhelpful direction, which might be harmful for athletic well-being and performance in the long run. Education and awareness of the impact of leader behaviour are important. And with these leaders, architects will emerge: members of the team who will embody the culture and lead alongside the coaches to create a sustainable high-performance culture.

It's not easy to bring cultural change at a team level, you will face various challenges and learn something new every time, but that's okay, because at the end of the day, two steps forward and one step back is still one step forward.

## Appendix A: Psychological safety checklist

- ☐ Team members often share their genuine thoughts and opinions without fear of judgment.
- ☐ Difficult conversations (release of players/staff, benching of players, etc.) are handled respectfully and constructively.
- ☐ Active listening is practiced and encouraged in discussions.
- ☐ Team members are honest with and supportive of each other, even when results are not in favour.
- ☐ Mistakes (including multiple similar mistakes, highly consequential mistakes) are treated as learning opportunities rather than punishable offenses.
- ☐ Individuals admit they don't know something without fear of negative consequences.
- ☐ Team members demonstrate empathy and encouragement.
- ☐ Team members feel included regardless of their background, identity, or experience level.
- ☐ There is mutual respect, even in disagreements.
- ☐ Microaggressions, bias, or exclusionary behaviours are addressed respectfully when they arise.
- ☐ People feel comfortable asking for help or feedback.
- ☐ Feedback is given constructively and respectfully.
- ☐ Accountability is encouraged along with safety in a balanced manner.

- ☐ Leaders model vulnerability by openly admitting mistakes or seeking input.
- ☐ There is transparency in decision-making.
- ☐ The team sticks through the highs and lows together.

***Note: This can be used as a Likert-type scale tool complemented by some qualitative questions if used as a survey tool across the team/organisation.***

## Note from Dr. Harini Priyadharshini Muralidharan

As a sports medicine specialist and the co-founder of a multidisciplinary team that has an incredible sports psychologist at the helm of affairs alongside me, I have seen firsthand the transformative power of an integrated sports science team. Among the various disciplines that contribute to the holistic well-being and performance of athletes, sports psychology stands out as a pivotal component. The role of sports psychology within a multidisciplinary team is essential for optimising athletes' mental resilience, focus, and overall performance.

When applied appropriately, psychological interventions have historically proven their undeniable impact on pushing the boundaries of human capabilities. In this article, I outline a few areas where this impact has been clearly measured.

### Mental Resilience and Stress Management

Athletes often face immense pressure to perform at their peak, which can lead to anxiety, stress, and burnout. Sports psychologists play a crucial role in helping athletes develop mental resilience and coping mechanisms. By teaching techniques such as visualisation, relaxation exercises, and cognitive-behavioural strategies, sports psychologists equip athletes with the tools to manage stress effectively. This mental fortitude not only enhances performance but also reduces the risk of injury, as a calm and focused mind is less prone to mistakes that could lead to physical harm.

### Focus and Concentration

In high-stakes competitions, an athlete's ability to maintain focus and concentration can be the difference between victory and defeat. Sports psychologists work with athletes to develop routines and mental strategies that sharpen their concentration. Techniques such as goal setting, mindfulness, and attentional control help athletes stay present and focused during critical moments. This enhanced mental acuity is invaluable, especially in sports that require split-second decisions and precise execution.

### Injury Rehabilitation and Recovery

The psychological aspect of injury rehabilitation is often overlooked, yet it is a critical component of the recovery process. Sports psychologists provide emotional support and motivation to injured athletes, helping them navigate the emotional rollercoaster of recovery. Through counselling and mental training, sports psychologists assist athletes in maintaining a positive outlook, setting realistic goals, and staying committed to their rehabilitation programs, which can be quite a mentally taxing period. The effects of these interventions continually impress our own team at The Performance Doctor, as we witness how psychological support significantly expedites the healing process and improves overall outcomes.

### Team Dynamics and Communication

In team sports, the dynamics between players can have a profound impact on performance. Sports psychologists work with teams to foster effective communication, trust, and cohesion among teammates. By addressing conflicts, enhancing group dynamics, and promoting a positive team culture, sports psychologists contribute to a harmonious and productive team environment. This collaborative atmosphere translates to better on-field performance and a stronger sense of camaraderie.

## Holistic Athlete Development

Ultimately, the integration of sports psychology into a multidisciplinary sports science team contributes to the holistic development of athletes. By addressing the mental and emotional aspects of sports, athletes are empowered to achieve their full potential. This comprehensive approach not only enhances athletic performance but also promotes overall well-being, paving the way for long-term success both on and off the field.

In conclusion, sports psychology is an indispensable element of a multidisciplinary sports science team. From mental resilience and focus to injury recovery and team dynamics, the contributions of sports psychologists are vital in nurturing well-rounded and high-performing athletes. As a sports medicine specialist, I strongly advocate for the inclusion of sports psychology in our holistic approach to athlete care and development.

### About Dr. Harini

Harini Priyadharshini Muralidharan is a dynamic professional with a passion for sports medicine and team management. She currently serves as the Team Manager and Doctor for the RCB Women's team, where she combines her expertise in sports medicine with team operations. Harini is also the Founder and Director of The Performance Doctor, an initiative dedicated to prehab and rehab, ensuring athletes are physically prepared for peak performance while managing injury prevention and recovery.

With a deep understanding of anti-doping regulations and sports operations, Harini brings a holistic approach to athlete care, focusing not just on performance but on long-term health and well-being. Her leadership extends to team management, where she works closely with athletes to optimize their physical and mental readiness for competition. Her work spans across the sports world, where she supports both individual athletes and teams in reaching their full potential.

## Note from Dr. Chirag Thonse

Integrating Psychological Principles into Sports Injury Management: An Indian Surgeon's Perspective

### Introduction

In the dynamic and competitive world of sports, injuries are a well-known and expected risk. The challenge today lies not only in overcoming the physical challenge and making the athlete competition-worthy again, but also in ensuring that he/she is psychologically ready to compete and face opponents on diverse and ruthless platforms.

Mind over matter, a game spells victory when both the mental and physical faculties come together to meet the best possible outcome for athletes at their potential best.

As an arthroscopic surgeon of 2 decades and having treated sportsmen for injuries from diverse fields and backgrounds in India, I have pulsed time and again the pressing need to address not only the physical aspects of sports injuries but also the psychological factors that play a crucial role in recovery. The mental makeup and emotional well-being of athletes significantly influence their rehabilitation outcomes. Understanding and integrating psychological principles into injury management is essential in creating a comprehensive approach that fosters not only physical healing but also mental fortitude.

However, the focus has traditionally been on the physical rehabilitation process, often neglecting the psychological impact of injuries. This oversight can lead to incomplete recovery, prolonged rehabilitation periods, and even premature retirement from sports. By incorporating psychological support into injury management, we can ensure a more holistic recovery process, enabling athletes to return to their sport with confidence and grit.

A well-woven and strong emotionally cognitive dimension adapted into rehabilitation can build resilience for the future, where challenges will always lurk but come with the credence to overcome.

**My Experience in the Field of Sports Psychology:**

Having worked in the field of sports injuries for several years, I have had the privilege of witnessing the discipline's evolution in India. When I first began, many athletes and coaches were sceptical about the value of psychological support in sports. The prevailing belief was that success was solely determined by physical training and technical skills. However, over time, I have seen a notable shift, with athletes, coaches, and administrators increasingly recognizing the importance of mental resilience, focus, emotional regulation, and team dynamics in enhancing performance.

The variety of sports in India provides a unique backdrop for this exploration. From cricket to kabaddi, wrestling, and badminton, each sport presents its own set of challenges when it comes to integrating psychological support. For example, in cricket, where the pressure is immense and often felt on a global stage, mental conditioning becomes critical. In contrast, sports like wrestling, where athletes often come from smaller towns and villages, require consideration of cultural factors and the social environment, which shape an athlete's mindset and approach to training.

Working with athletes from diverse backgrounds, regions, and sports has underscored the importance of tailoring psychological practices to meet the specific needs of each athlete, their sport's requirements, and cultural context.

A one-size-fits-all approach is rarely effective, and this is one of the key lessons I've learned through my career.

**Common Psychological Challenges Faced by Athletes**

1. Injuries can trigger a multitude of psychological challenges for athletes, which, if not addressed, can hinder their recovery and performance, including:
2. Anxiety: Many athletes experience heightened anxiety regarding recovery timelines, performance expectations, and the fear of being sidelined from competition. This anxiety can be particularly acute in a competitive sports environment like India, where expectations can be immense. The pressure to perform and the fear of losing one's place in the team can exacerbate anxiety, leading to a negative impact on the recovery process
3. Depression: The loss of identity and purpose, of not playing the field that often accompanies an injury, can lead to feelings of depression. Athletes may struggle with isolation and a sense of disconnect from their game, affecting their overall mental health. Depression can manifest as a lack of motivation, withdrawal from social interactions, and a general sense of hopelessness, all of which can impede the rehabilitation process.

Fear of Re-Injury: Kinesiophobia, or the fear of re-injury, is a significant barrier that can inhibit athletes from fully engaging in their rehabilitation. This fear can manifest in the hesitation to return to the sport, which may prolong the recovery process and create an unconscious but nasty sense of escapism. Athletes may become overly cautious, avoiding certain movements or exercises, which could delay their return to complete fitness.

## Opportunities from Incorporating Psychological Support

1. The integration of physio and psychotherapy into injury recovery programs offers various opportunities to enhance the overall recovery process.:
2. Enhanced Motivation: Psychological interventions instil a sense of purpose and motivation in athletes. Techniques like goal setting and visualization can empower individuals to stay committed to their rehabilitation, fostering a proactive mindset. By setting achievable goals and visualizing successful outcomes, athletes can maintain their focus and drive through the recovery process. Improved Adherence to Rehabilitation Protocols: By addressing psychological barriers, athletes can better adhere to prescribed rehabilitation protocols. Mental health support can facilitate a more positive approach to recovery, making it easier for athletes to engage
3. fully in their physical therapy. When athletes understand the importance of each step in their rehabilitation and feel supported psychologically, they are more likely to follow through with their treatment plans.

Resilience: Incorporating psychological strategies can help athletes build resilience, enabling them to cope with setbacks and challenges throughout their recovery journey. Resilience is a critical factor in overcoming the mental and emotional hurdles that come with injuries. By developing coping mechanisms and a positive mindset, athletes can better navigate the ups and downs of the recovery process.

## Case Studies Demonstrating Successful Integration

1. Several case studies highlight the successful integration of psychological principles in injury management, showcasing the positive impact of a holistic approach:

2. Indian Cricketer's Recovery: A prominent Indian cricketer facing a knee injury underwent a comprehensive rehabilitation program that included psychological support. A sports psychologist worked with him to address his anxiety and fear of re-injury. Through cognitive restructuring and mindfulness techniques, he not only adhered to his rehabilitation but also returned to the pitch with renewed confidence and performance. The cricketer reported feeling more mentally prepared to handle the pressures of the game and was able to perform at his best upon returning to the field.

Wrestler's Mental Resilience: An Indian wrestler who suffered a shoulder injury benefited from a program that combined physical therapy with psychological interventions. By utilising visualisation strategies to mentally rehearse his return to the mat, he overcame his fears and made a successful comeback, illustrating the power of a holistic approach. The wrestler credited his mental preparation as a key factor in his ability to return to competition with confidence and strength.

**Examples from Indian Sports Bodies**

In India, organisations like the Sports Authority of India (SAI) and various national sports federations have begun recognising the importance of mental health in sports. The SAI has initiated programs that provide mental health resources, including access to sports psychologists, to athletes across disciplines.

For instance, the Indian Women's Cricket Team has incorporated mental health support as an integral part of their training regime, focusing on building mental resilience alongside physical skills. This comprehensive approach has contributed to their recent successes on the international stage.

The team's management has emphasised the importance of mental well-being, providing regular access to sports psychologists and mental health workshops to ensure that players are mentally prepared for the challenges of competitive cricket.

**Recommendations for Sports Organisations and Medical Professionals**

1. To effectively incorporate psychological strategies into injury management, sports organisations and medical professionals in India should consider the following recommendations:
2. Cross-functional Partnership: Foster collaboration among sports medicine professionals, psychologists, and coaches to create a comprehensive recovery program that addresses both physical and psychological needs. A team-based approach ensures that all aspects of an athlete's recovery are considered, leading to more effective outcomes.
3. Education and Training: Provide training for coaches and sports trainers on recognizing psychological challenges and the importance of mental health in injury recovery. Educating the support staff about the psychological impact of injuries can help them better understand and support their athletes.
4. Access to Mental Health Resources: Ensure that athletes have access to qualified sports psychologists who can deliver tailored mental health interventions during rehabilitation. Having a dedicated mental health professional on the team can make a significant difference in an athlete's recovery journey.
5. Routine Psychological Assessments: Implement regular psychological evaluations as part of the rehabilitation process to identify mental health challenges early and adapt recovery plans accordingly. Early detection of psychological issues can prevent them from escalating and impacting the recovery process.

6. Promote Open Communication: Encourage a culture of openness around mental health within teams, reducing stigma and normalizing discussions about psychological well-being. Creating an environment where athletes feel comfortable discussing their mental health can lead to more effective support and intervention.

## Conclusion

The integration of psychological principles into sports injury management is crucial for fostering a holistic recovery process in athletes. By addressing the psychological challenges they face, we enhance motivation, adherence to rehabilitation, and overall mental wellness. As we move forward, the future of sports medicine in India will hinge on our ability to treat athletes comprehensively—physically and psychologically. This integration not only prepares them for healthier recoveries but also equips them with the mental skills necessary for sustained success in their sporting careers. Through continued efforts, we can create an environment where mental health is prioritised, leading to a new era of athlete care and performance in India.

By embracing a multidisciplinary approach that includes psychological support, we can ensure that athletes are not only physically prepared to return to their sport but also mentally resilient to face the challenges that come with it. This holistic approach will not only improve recovery outcomes but also contribute to the overall well-being and longevity of athletes' careers. As we continue to advance in the field of sports medicine, the integration of psychological principles will be a cornerstone of athlete care, paving the way for a healthier, more resilient generation of sports professionals in India.

**About Dr. Chirag**

Dr. Chirag Thonse is a senior orthopedic surgeon with 14 years of experience, specializing in sports injuries, arthroscopy, and joint replacement surgeries. He has performed over 10,000 surgeries, including 7,000 arthroscopic ACL surgeries and 3,000 joint replacement procedures. Dr. Thonse is committed to providing quality, patient-centered orthopedic care, addressing a wide range of sports-related injuries and orthopedic conditions.

Active in education, he has trained over 250 orthopedic surgeons and mentored more than 75 professionals from across the globe. Dr. Thonse is a core committee member of the Indian Orthopaedic Research Group and regularly contributes to national and international conferences, delivering over 400 lectures and cadaveric courses.

A faculty member for over 350 conferences, Dr. Thonse has pioneered the Bengaluru Arthroscopic Course and contributes chapters to key orthopedic textbooks. He is also an editorial board member for several renowned journals, including the *Journal of Arthroscopy & Sports Medicine.*

## Note from Shiny Surendran

### The Nutrition - Mental Health Connection in Athletes: A Multidisciplinary Approach

Athletes are often judged by their physical endurance, strength, and agility, yet true success in sports depends on a seamless integration of both physical and mental well-being. Psychological resilience, focus, and motivation can make the difference between winning and losing. While sports psychology has traditionally centred on mental conditioning techniques, emerging research underscores how essential nutrition is in supporting mental health, underscoring that the two must be addressed together for peak performance.

Deficiencies in essential micronutrients, chronic inflammation, and food intolerances can lead to mood disturbances, cognitive decline, and symptoms resembling anxiety or depression. To provide athletes with comprehensive support, a multidisciplinary team consisting of sports psychologists, nutritionists, and medical professionals must work together. This integrated, a holistic approach ensures that both mental and nutritional aspects are addressed simultaneously, optimising performance through a seamless balance of mind and body.

### Micronutrient Deficiencies and Their Role in Mental Health

Certain vitamins and minerals play a direct role in brain function, neurotransmitter production, and emotional stability. When athletes lack these essential nutrients, they may experience symptoms such as fatigue, irritability, poor concentration, and mood fluctuations.

- Key Micronutrients for Psychological **Resilience**
- **Vitamin B12 & B-Complex:** These vitamins are essential for energy metabolism and brain health. A deficiency can lead to fatigue, memory problems, and depressive symptoms. Vegan or

vegetarian athletes are particularly at risk due to limited dietary sources of B12.

- **Vitamin D3:** Low levels of vitamin D3 have been associated with depression, low energy, and weakened immune function. Athletes training indoors or in regions with limited sunlight exposure may benefit from supplementation.
- **Magnesium:** This mineral plays a crucial role in relaxation, stress reduction, and sleep quality. Magnesium depletion—common in athletes due to sweat loss—can contribute to anxiety, muscle cramps, and restlessness.
- **Omega-3 Fatty Acids:** These healthy fats support cognitive function, emotional stability, and inflammation reduction. Low omega-3 intake has been linked to mood imbalances and increased stress levels.
- **Iron:** Essential for oxygen transport, iron deficiency—especially in female athletes—can cause fatigue, dizziness, and mood swings.

### Case Example: An Endurance Runner's Struggle with Low Energy

A 30-year-old endurance runner experienced persistent low motivation, irritability, and chronic fatigue. Blood tests revealed deficiencies in B12 and iron, which were impairing oxygen delivery and neurological function. After dietary adjustments and supplementation, the athlete noticed significant improvements in energy levels and mental clarity within a few weeks.

This case underscores the importance of routine nutritional assessments in athlete mental health management.

## Inflammation and Its Impact on Mental Performance

Chronic inflammation is increasingly recognised as a contributing factor to depression, anxiety, and cognitive decline. Athletes, particularly those engaged in high-intensity training, exhibit elevated inflammatory markers that can impair cognitive function and mood. This further demonstrates how managing inflammation through proper nutrition is vital for maintaining a resilient mindset and optimal performance.

- How Inflammation Affects the **Brain**
- Inflammatory responses release cytokines, which can disrupt neurotransmitter balance, leading to brain fog, irritability, and emotional instability.

**Chronic inflammation has been linked to conditions such as major depressive disorder (MDD) and cognitive fatigue.**

- Pro-Inflammatory vs. Anti-Inflammatory **Foods**
- **Increase:** Omega-3-rich fish, leafy greens, turmeric, ginger, berries, nuts, and seeds

Reduce: Processed foods, trans fats, refined sugar, excessive caffeine, and artificial additives

## Monitoring Inflammation for Mental Resilience

Athletes can assess their inflammation levels through C-reactive protein (CRP) tests. Sports psychologists and nutritionists can then create personalized anti-inflammatory strategies, helping to enhance both physical recovery and cognitive function.

Unrecognised food intolerances and sensitivities can lead to chronic inflammation, gut disturbances, and neurotransmitter imbalances. These issues may manifest as anxiety, brain fog, irritability, and mood swings, affecting performance.

### Common Food Sensitivities That Impact Mental Health

- **Gluten & Dairy:** Some athletes experience brain fog, fatigue, and mood fluctuations after consuming gluten or dairy, possibly due to an immune response.
- **Anti-Nutrients:** Certain foods contain compounds (e.g., phytic acid, oxalates) that block the absorption of essential minerals, leading to deficiencies.
- **Histamine-Rich Foods:** Fermented foods, cured meats, and aged cheeses can trigger anxiety, sleep disturbances, and headaches in sensitive individuals.

### Case Example: A Tennis Player's Mental Clarity Breakthrough

A professional tennis player struggled with anxiety, poor concentration, and performance inconsistencies. Despite mental training, his symptoms persisted. Further evaluation revealed gluten intolerance, leading to chronic gut inflammation. After eliminating gluten and incorporating probiotics, his anxiety decreased, and his cognitive sharpness improved.

This case highlights the importance of integrating nutrition and psychological support for peak performance.

### A Multidisciplinary Approach: The Road Ahead for Athlete Mental Health

Athletes need more than just mental coaching or physical training they require a comprehensive approach that integrates psychology, nutrition, and medical insights. A multidisciplinary team ensures that athletes receive personalized interventions that optimise both mind and body.

The connection between nutrition and sports psychology is undeniable. By addressing micronutrient deficiencies, inflammation, and food intolerances, we can move beyond traditional mental training methods and adopt a truly holistic approach.

In conclusion, a truly multidisciplinary strategy, where psychologists, nutritionists, and medical professionals work in synergy, ensures that athletes receive the best possible care for both mental and physical well-being. By prioritising this integrated approach, we empower athletes to unlock their full potential, reaffirming that nutrition and mental health are two sides of the same coin in achieving peak performance.

**About Shiny**

Shiny Surendran is one of India's leading sports nutritionists, internationally recognized for her expertise in optimizing athletic performance. She was the first Indian to earn the Graduate Diploma in Sports Nutrition from the International Olympic Committee, and she holds certifications as a Level 2 ISAK Kinanthropometrist (New Zealand) and an Accredited Sports Dietitian (Sports Dietitians Australia). With specializations in sports nutrition, preventive nutrition, kinanthropometry, and nutrigenomics, Shiny has worked with hundreds of athletes worldwide — from elite international competitors to rising young talent — helping them enhance performance and manage complex nutrition-related challenges. Her guidance has also extended to celebrities, recreational athletes, and individuals facing health concerns such as obesity, PCOS, cardiovascular disease, diabetes, food intolerances, and infertility.

Through her evidence-based and athlete-centric approach, Shiny continues to champion holistic health and performance, shaping the future of sports nutrition in India and beyond.

# EDITOR'S NOTE

Working on this book has been an enriching journey, both professionally and personally. With a background in athletics and a deep interest in the field of sports psychology, I approached the content with curiosity and a learner's lens.

What stood out most was the diversity of perspectives offered by each author. Observing their unique styles of writing and ways of communicating complex ideas made the editorial process both insightful and fulfilling.

One of my main focuses was to ensure the content remained clear, accessible, and relevant to a wide audience — including athletes, coaches, parents, and professionals. This required regularly shifting perspectives, which challenged me to think more broadly about the field and its real-world impact.

As an athlete myself, reading and working through these topics felt familiar — like revisiting challenges I've faced on the field: battling doubt, staying focused, pushing through setbacks. It reminded me that the mental game is just as real and demanding as the physical one. Through my own journey, I've seen how awareness and application of sports psychology practices could have significantly changed the way I approached my sport and my personal limitations. Had I known these techniques earlier, I believe they would have helped me manage pressure and build resilience in ways that would've positively impacted both my performance and mindset.

Editing this book wasn't just an exercise in clarity; it became a reflection on my own journey and how much strength truly comes from within.

It's been a privilege to contribute to a work that highlights the transformative power of sports psychology in both athletic performance and overall well-being.

**– Sampritha Arrchana**

# REFERENCES


**Chapter 2 - Implementation of a psychosocial sport psychology programme with tribal athletes**

Harwood, C. G. (2008). Developmental consulting in a professional football academy: The 5Cs coaching efficacy program. The Sport Psychologist, 22(1), 109–133. https://doi.org/10.1123/tsp. 22.1.109

**Chapter 3 - Perfectionism in Sport and Its Manifestation**

Dieter H. & Schinke, R. (2020). *The Routledge International Encyclopedia of Sport and Exercise Psychology: Volume 1: Theoretical and Methodological Concepts.* Routledge, London

Fleming, D. & Dorsch, T. (2024): "There's no good, it's just satisfactory": perfectionism, performance, and perfectionistic reactivity in NCAA student-athletes, *International Journal of Sport and Exercise Psychology*, DOI: 10.1080/1612197X.2024.2410282

Flett, G. & Hewitt, P. (2005). The Perils of Perfectionism in Sports and Exercise. *Current Directions in Psychological Science,* Vol. 14

Flett, G. L., & Hewitt, P. L. (2016). Reflections on perfection and the pressure to be perfect in athletes, dancers, and exercisers: A focus on perfectionistic reactivity in key situations and life contexts. In A. P. Hill (Ed.),

The psychology of perfectionism in sport, dance, and exercise (pp. 312–336). Routledge Gotwals, J., Stoeber, J., Dunn, J. & Stoll, O. (2012). Are Perfectionistic Strivings in Sport Adaptive? A Systematic Review of Confirmatory, Contradictory, and Mixed Evidence. *Canadian Psychology,* 53 (4), 263-279

Gotwals, J. K., & Dunn, J. (2009). A multi-method multi-analytic approach to establishing internal construct validity evidence: The Sport Multidimensional Perfectionism Scale 2. *Measurement in Physical Education and Exercise Science, 13*(2), 71–92. https://doi.org/10.1080/10913670902812663

Hewitt, P., Flett, G., Sherry, S., Habke, M., Parkin, M., Lam, R., McMurthy, B., Ediger, E., Fairlie, P., & Stein, M. (2003). The Interpersonal Expression of Perfection:

Perfectionistic Self-Presentation and Psychological Distress. *Journal of Personality and Social Psychology,* 84 (6). 1303-1325

Hill, A., Jowett, & Howard, S. (2017). Perfectionism in Sport, Dance, and Exercise: Theory, Research, Applications. Routledge

Hill, A. P., Mallinson-Howard, S. H., & Jowett, G. E. (2018). Perfectionism in Sport: A meta-analytical review. *Sport, Exercise, and Performance Psychology*, Vol. 7 (3)

Hill A. P., Madigan D. J., Jowett G. E. (2020). Perfectionism and athlete engagement: A multi-sample test of the 2 × 2 model of perfectionism. *Psychology of Sport and Exercise*, 48, 101664. https://doi.org/10.1016/j.psychsport.2020.101664

Hill, A., Madigan, D., Curran, T., Jowett, G, & Rumbold, J. (2024). Exploring and Evaluating the Two-Factor Model of Perfectionism in Sport. *Journal of Psychoeducational Assessment*, Vol. 42(6), 612–634

**Chapter 5 - 'You will fail, fail better': Sporting Resilience for adapting to adversity and failure**

Ding, X., Fang, H., Liu, Y., Zheng, L., Zhu, X., Duan, H., & Wu, J. (2022). Neurocognitive correlates of psychological resilience: Event-related potential studies. Journal of Affective Disorders, 312, 100-106.

Fletcher, D., & Sarkar, M. (2013). Psychological resilience. European Psychologist.

Fletcher, D., & Sarkar, M. (2016). Mental fortitude training: An evidence-based approach tdeveloping psychological resilience for sustained success. Journal of Sport Psychology in Action, 7(3), 135-157.

Galli, N., & Gonzalez, S. P. (2015). Psychological resilience in sport: A review of the literature and implications for research and practice. International Journal of Sport and Exercise Psychology, 13(3), 243-257.

Gonzalez, S. P., Detling, N., & Galli, N. A. (2016). Case studies of developing resilience in elite sport: Applying theory to guide interventions. Journal of Sport Psychology in Action, 7(3), 158-169.

Gucciardi, D. F., Jackson, B., Coulter, T. J., & Mallett, C. J. (2011). The Connor-Davidson Resilience Scale (CD-RISC): Dimensionality and age-related measurement invariance with Australian cricketers. Psychology of Sport and Exercise, 12(4), 423-433.

Gupta, S., & McCarthy, P. J. (2021). Sporting resilience during COVID-19: What is the nature of this adversity, and how are competitive elite athletes adapting? Frontiers in Psychology, 12, 611261.

Gupta, S., & McCarthy, P. J. (2022). The sporting resilience model: A systematic review of resilience in sport performers. Frontiers in Psychology, 13, 1003053.

Gupta, S., & McCarthy, P. J. (2024). "You don't get resilience overnight": A grounded theory framework of the ARC sporting resilience development. Discover Psychology, 4(1), 72.

Gupta, S., & Reddy, K. J. (2023). Positive people and confident competitors: Resilient youth development through sport and physical activity. In Handbook of Youth Development: Policies and Perspectives from India and Beyond (pp. 165-191). Springer Nature Singapore.

Hill, Y., Den Hartigh, R. J., Meijer, R. R., De Jonge, P., & Van Yperen, N. W. (2018). The temporal process of resilience. Sport and Exercise Psychology Review

Luthar, S. S., & Cicchetti, D. (2000). The construct of resilience: Implications for interventions and social policies. Development and Psychopathology, 12(4), 857-885.

Luthar, S. S., Sawyer, J. A., & Brown, P. J. (2006). Conceptual issues in studies of resilience: Past, present, and future research. Annals of the New York Academy of Sciences, 1094(1), 105-115.

Masten, A. S. (2014). Ordinary magic. Resilience in development. Guilford Publications.

Mellalieu, S. D., Neil, R., Hanton, S., & Fletcher, D. (2009). Competition stress in sport performers: Stressors experienced in the competition environment. Journal of Sports Sciences, 27(7), 729-744.

Papathomas, A., & Lavallee, D. (2012). Narrative constructions of anorexia and abuse: An athlete's search for meaning in trauma. Journal of Loss and Trauma, 17(4), 293-318.

Podlog, L., & Eklund, R. C. (2006). A longitudinal investigation of competitive athletes' return to sport following serious injury. Journal of Applied Sport Psychology, 18(1), 44-68.

Wagstaff, C. R., Sarkar, M., Davidson, C. L., & Fletcher, D. (2016). Resilience in sport: A critical review of psychological processes, sociocultural influences, and organisational dynamics. In The Organisational Psychology of Sport (pp. 138-168).

**Chapter 6 - Nurturing the Nurturers**

Brown, B. (2015). *Daring greatly: How the courage to be vulnerable transforms the way we live, love, parent, and lead.* Penguin.

Cameron, J. (2002). *The artist's way: A spiritual path to higher creativity* (10th anniv. ed.). Jeremy P. Tarcher/Putnam.

David, S. (2016). *Emotional agility: Get unstuck, embrace change, and thrive in work and life.* Avery.

Figley, C. R. (2002). Compassion fatigue: Psychotherapists' chronic lack of self-care. *Journal of Clinical Psychology, 58*(11), 1433-1441. https://doi.org/10.1002/jclp.10090

Hatfield, E., Cacioppo, J. T., & Rapson, R. L. (1994). *Emotional contagion.*

Cambridge University Press.

Kabat-Zinn, J. (1990). *Full catastrophe living: Using the wisdom of your body and mind to face stress, pain, and illness.* Delacorte Press.

Luthar, S. S., Cicchetti, D., & Becker, B. (2000). The construct of resilience: A critical evaluation and guidelines for future work. *Child Development, 71*(3), 543-562. https://doi.org/10.1111/1467-8624.00164

Morrissette, P. J. (2001). Reducing burnout in counselors. *Journal of Employment Counseling, 38*(2), 82-87. https://doi.org/10.1002/j.2161-1920.2001.tb00491.x

Neff, K. D., & Germer, C. K. (2013). A pilot study and randomized controlled trial of the mindful self-compassion program. *Journal of Clinical Psychology, 69*(1), 28-44. https://doi.org/10.1002/jclp.21923

Schieman, S., & Glavin, P. (2008). Trouble at the border? Gender, flexibility at work, and the work-home interface. *Social Problems, 55*(4), 590-611. https://doi.org/10.1525/sp.2008.55.4.590

Shapiro, S. L., Schwartz, G. E., & Bonner, G. (1998). Effects of mindfulness-based stress reduction on medical and premedical students. *Journal of Behavioral Medicine, 21*(6), 581-599. https://doi.org/10.1023/A:1018700829825

Taylor, S. E. (2011). Social support: A review. In H. S. Friedman (Ed.), *The Oxford handbook of health psychology*(pp 189-214). Oxford University Press.

**Chapter 7 - Gender Inclusivity in Sport**

Abad-Santos, A. (2024, August 1). Discrimination against trans olympians has roots in Nazi Germany. Vox. https://www.vox.com/culture/364032/trans-athletes-olympics-2024

Dutee Chand cleared to race as IAAF suspends 'gender test' rules. (2015, July 27). BBC Sport. https://www.bbc.com/sport/athletics/33683779

Macur, J. (2014, October 7). Fighting for the Body She Was Born With. The New York Times. https://www.nytimes.com/2014/10/07/sports/sprinter-dutee-chand-fights- ban-over-her-testosterone-level.html

Misri, D. (2019, May 28). Why Dutee Chand's 'coming out' is more complicated than it seems. Al Jazeera. https://www.aljazeera.com/opinions/2019/5/28/why-dutee-chands-comin g-out-is-more-complicated-than-it-seems

Pape, M. (2019). Expertise and non-binary bodies: Sex, gender and the case of Dutee Chand. Body & Society, 25(4), 3-28. https://doi.org/10.1177/1357034x19865940

Santhi 'medal should be returned. (2009). BBC News. https://news.bbc.co.uk/2/hi/south_asia/8253880.stm

Tjønndal, A. (2024, August 10) Imane Khelif: The Algerian boxer who overcame an ugly gender furore to win Olympic gold. The Conversation. https://theconversation.com/imane-khelif-the-algerian-boxer-who-overcame-an-ugly-gender-furore-to-win-olympic-gold-236175

Caster Samenya, Running in a Body That's My Own, New York Times, Oct 21, 2023

Malhotra K, Transgenderism In Sports In India: Current Legal Position And Analysis, Jul 17, 2023

https://www.g-spr.com/post/transgenderism-in-sports-in-india-current-legal-position-and-analysis

https://www.popsci.com/story/science/testosterone-effect-athletic-per formance/

Balthazar, C. H., Garcia, M. C., & Spadari-Bratfisch, R. C. (2012).

Salivary concentrations of cortisol and testosterone and prediction of performance in a professional triathlon competition. Stress, 15(5), 495–502. https://doi.org/10.3109/10253890.2011.642033

Bermon S, Garnier PSerum androgen levels and their relation to performance in track and field: mass spectrometry results from 2127 observations in male and female elite athletes British Journal of Sports Medicine 2017;51:1309-1314.

Is testosterone responsible for athletic success in female athletes? Ildus I. Ahmetov, Thomas R. Roos, Albina A. Stepanova, Elnara M. Biktagirova, Ekaterina A. Semenova, Irina S. Shchuplova, Larisa V. Bets bioRxiv 557348; doi: https://doi.org/10.1101/557348

Now published in The Journal of Sports Medicine and Physical Fitness doi: 10.23736/S0022-4707.20.10171-3

Sönksen, P.H., Holt, R.I.G., Böhning, W. et al. Why do endocrine profiles in elite athletes differ between sports?. Clin Diabetes Endocrinol 4, 3 (2018). https://doi.org/10.1186/s40842-017-0050-3

Abad-Santos, A. (2024, August 1). Discrimination against trans olympians has roots in Nazi Germany. Vox.

https://www.vox.com/culture/364032/trans-athletes-olympics-2024

Dutee Chand cleared to race as IAAF suspends 'gender test' rules. (2015, July 27). BBC Sport. https://www.bbc.com/sport/athletics/33683779

Macur, J. (2014, October 7). Fighting for the Body She Was Born With. The New York Times. https://www.nytimes.com/2014/10/07/sports/sprinter-dutee-chand-fights- ban-over-her-testosterone-level.html

Misri, D. (2019, May 28). Why Dutee Chand's 'coming out' is more complicated than it seems. Al Jazeera. https://www.aljazeera.com/opinions/2019/5/28/why-dutee-chands-comin g-out-is-more-complicated-than-it-seems

Pape, M. (2019). Expertise and non-binary bodies: Sex, gender and the case of Dutee Chand. Body & Society, 25(4), 3-28. https://doi.org/10.1177/1357034x19865940

Santhi 'medal should be returned. (2009). BBC News. https://news.bbc.co.uk/2/hi/south_asia/8253880.stm

Tjønndal, A. (2024, August 10). Imane Khelif: The Algerian boxer who overcame an ugly gender furore to win Olympic gold. The Conversation. https://theconversation.com/imane-khelif-the-algerian-boxer-who-overcame-an-ugly-gender-furore-to-win-olympic-gold-236175

Caster Samenya, Running in a Body That's My Own, New York Times, Oct 21, 2023

Malhotra K, Transgenderism In Sports In India: Current Legal Position And Analysis, Jul 17, 2023

https://www.g-spr.com/post/transgenderism-in-sports-in-india-current-legal-position-and-analysis

https://www.popsci.com/story/science/testosterone-effect-athletic-per formance/

Balthazar, C. H., Garcia, M. C., & Spadari-Bratfisch, R. C. (2012). Salivary concentrations of cortisol and testosterone and prediction of performance in a professional triathlon competition. Stress, 15(5), 495–502. https://doi.org/10.3109/10253890.2011.642033

Bermon S, Garnier PSerum androgen levels and their relation to performance in track and field: mass spectrometry results from 2127

observations in male and female elite athletesBritish. Journal of Sports Medicine 2017;51:1309-1314.

Is testosterone responsible for athletic success in female athletes? Ildus I. Ahmetov, Thomas R. Roos, Albina A. Stepanova, Elnara M. Biktagirova, Ekaterina A. Semenova, Irina S. Shchuplova, Larisa V. Bets bioRxiv 557348; doi: https://doi.org/10.1101/557348

Now published in The Journal of Sports Medicine and Physical Fitness doi: 10.23736/S0022-4707.20.10171-3

Sönksen, P.H., Holt, R.I.G., Böhning, W. et al. Why do endocrine profiles in elite athletes differ between sports?. Clin Diabetes Endocrinol 4, 3 (2018). https://doi.org/10.1186/s40842-017-0050-3

**Chapter 8 - Sport performance & Unconscious processes Jung, C.G. (1974). Dreams. Princeton University Press.**

Jung, C. G. (1963). Memories, dreams, reflections. Crown Publishing Group/ Random House.

Hellinger, B. (2008). Rising in Love: A Philosophy of Being.Hellinger Publications.

**Chapter 10 - Field Of Potential: The Emerging Flow State**

Harwood, C. (2008). Developmental consulting in a professional football academy: The 5Cs coaching efficacy program. *The Sport Psychologist*, *22*, 109-133

Harwood, C.G. & Anderson, R. (2015). *Coaching psychological skills in youth football: Developing the 5Cs.* Bennion-Kearney Publishers.

Hauser, L., Harwood, C.G., Honer, O., O'Connor, D. & Wachsmuth, S. (2022). Talent Development Environments within Sports: A Scoping Review examining Functional and Dysfunctional Environmental Features. *International Review of Sport and Exercise Psychology.* Advanced online publication

Martindale, R. J., Collins, D., & Daubney, J. (2005). Talent development: A guide for practice and research within sport. Quest, 57(4), 353-375

**Chapter 12 - Sleep and sport in the Indian Context**

Barrett, R. S., & Francescutti, L. H. (2021). Hardwired: How Our Instincts to Be Healthy are Making Us Sick. Springer International Publishing. https://doi.org/10.1007/978-3-030-51729-8

Basu, N., Saxena, A., Sarraf, A., Singh, A., Gulani, A., Yadav, M., Panwar, S., Mathur, V., & Misra, R. (2013). A Cross-Sectional Questionnaire Based Study to Evaluate Subjective Sleep Quality among Undergraduate Students in India.

International Journal of Indian Psychology, October. https://doi.org/10.25215/0904.024

Castaldelli-Maia, J. M., Gallinaro, J. G. D. M. E., Falcão, R. S., Gouttebarge, V., Hitchcock, M. E., Hainline, B., Reardon, C. L., & Stull, T. (2019). Mental health symptoms and disorders in elite athletes: A systematic review on cultural influencers and barriers to athletes seeking treatment. British Journal of Sports Medicine, 53(11), 707–721.

https://doi.org/10.1136/bjsports-2019-100710

Charest, J., & Grandner, M. A. (2022). Sleep and Athletic Performance: Impacts on Physical Performance, Mental Performance, Injury Risk and Recovery, and Mental Health: An Update. Sleep Medicine Clinics, 17(2), 263–282. https://doi.org/10.1016/j.jsmc.2022.03.006

Chokroverty, S. (2017). Overview of Normal Sleep. In Sleep Disorders Medicine (Vol. 36, Issue 1, pp. 5–27). Springer New York. https://doi.org/10.1007/978-1-4939-6578-6_2

Datta, K., & Yadav, N. (2024). Sleep and sports. Sports Science in India: Practice and Perspective, 63–75. https://doi.org/10.4324/9781003477686-6 Grandner, M. A. (2017). Sleep, Health, and Society. In Sleep Medicine Clinics (Vol. 12, Issue 1, pp. 1–22). W.B. Saunders. https://doi.org/10.1016/j.jsmc.2016.10.012

Grandner, M. A., Ruiter Petrov, M. E., Rattanaumpawan, P., Jackson, N., Platt, A., & Patel, N. P. (2013). Sleep symptoms, race/ethnicity, and socioeconomic position. Journal of Clinical Sleep Medicine, 9(9), 897–905. https://doi.org/10.5664/jcsm.2990

Grandner, M. A., & Athey, A. B. (2024). Sleep and Sport: Physical Performance, Mental Performance, Injury Prevention, and Competitive Advantage for Athletes, Coaches, and Trainers. Academic Press.

Grewal, S., Theijse, R. T., Dunlop, G., van Deurzen, D. F. P., van den Bekerom, M. P. J., Klautz, R. J. M., Lefebvre, R. P., Munsami, D., & Grewal, N. (2024). Exploring the impact of sleep on emotional and physical well-being in professional cricketers: a cohort study over an in-season training period.

Frontiers in Sports and Active Living, 6(June), 2–8. https://doi.org/10.3389/fspor.2024.1389565

Guru, C. S., Datta, K., Krishnan, A., Kumar, A., Mahajan, U., Jhajharia, S., Kumar, M., Kumar, A., Yadav, N., & Singh, A. (2019). Sleep Pattern and Sports

Performance of Adolescent Archers: A Pre-Post-intervention Pilot Study. Sleep and Vigilance, 3(2), 143–149.

https://doi.org/10.1007/s41782-019-00073-5

Hobson, J. A. (2005). Sleep is of the brain, by the brain, and for the brain. Nature, 437(7063), 1254–1256. https://doi.org/10.1038/nature04283

Janse van Rensburg, D. C., Jansen van Rensburg, A., Fowler, P. M., Bender,

A. M., Stevens, D., Sullivan, K. O., Fullagar, H. H. K., Alonso, J. M., Biggins, M., Claassen-Smithers, A., Collins, R., Dohi, M., Driller, M. W., Dunican, I. C., Gupta, L., Halson, S. L., Lastella, M., Miles, K. H., Nedelec, M., … Botha, T. (2021). Managing Travel Fatigue and Jet Lag in Athletes: A Review and Consensus Statement. Sports Medicine, 51(10), 2029–2050. https://doi.org/10.1007/s40279-021-01502-0

Johnson, M. R. D. (2000). Perceptions of Barriers to Healthy Physical Activity among Asian Communities. Sport, Education and Society, 5(1), 51–70. https://doi.org/10.1080/135733200114433

Kalpana, K., Hussain, E., Bhati, P., Vatsala, S., & Khanna, G. L. (2022). Sleep Quality and Mental Health Status of Indian Male Kho Kho Players in a National Camp: A Cross-sectional Observational Study. Sleep and Vigilance, 6(1), 223–228. https://doi.org/10.1007/s41782-022-00206-3

Lastella, M., Memon, A. R., & Vincent, G. E. (2020). Global Research Output on Sleep Research in Athletes from 1966 to 2019: A Bibliometric Analysis.

Clocks and Sleep, 2(2), 99–119. https://doi.org/10.3390/clockssleep2020010
Ramanathan, S., & Crocker, P. R. E. (2009). The influence of family and culture on physical activity among female adolescents from the Indian diaspora. Qualitative Health Research, 19(4), 492–503. https://doi.org/10.1177/1049732309332651

Simpson, N. S., Gibbs, E. L., & Matheson, G. O. (2017). Optimising sleep to maximize performance: implications and recommendations for elite athletes. Scandinavian Journal of Medicine & Science in Sports, 27(3), 266–274. https://doi.org/10.1111/sms.12703

Taheri, M., & Arabameri, E. (2012). The effect of sleep deprivation on choice, Reaction time, and anaerobic power of college student athletes. Asian Journal of Sports Medicine, 3(1), 15–20. https://doi.org/10.5812/asjsm.34719

Toms, M., Dhingra, M., & Majumdar, P. (2024). Sports Science in India. In Sports Science in India. https://doi.org/10.4324/9781003477686

Van Rensburg, D. C. C. J., Fowler, P., & Racinais, S. (2021). Practical tips to manage travel fatigue and jet lag in athletes. British Journal of Sports Medicine, 55(15), 821–822. https://doi.org/10.1136/bjsports-2020-103163 Vlahoyiannis, A., Aphamis, G., Bogdanis, G. C., Sakkas, G. K., Andreou, E., & Giannaki, C. D. (2021). Deconstructing athletes' sleep: A systematic review of the influence of age, sex, athletic expertise, sport type, and season on sleep characteristics. Journal of Sport and Health Science, 10(4), 387–402. https://doi.org/10.1016/j.jshs.2020.03.006

[Duroflexworld]. (2023, June 1). Virat Kohli on being a world-class athlete. Virat Duroflex [Video]. Youtube. https://www.youtube.com/watch?v=LincR

**Chapter 14: Moulding the Inner Circle**

Maté, G. (2003). *When the body says no: The cost of hidden stress*. Wiley.

Porges, S. W. (2011). *The polyvagal theory: Neurophysiological foundations of emotions, attachment, communication, and self-regulation*. W.W. Norton & Company.

Hofstede, G., Hofstede, G. J., & Minkov, M. (2010). *Cultures and organisations: Software of the mind: Intercultural cooperation and its importance for survival*. McGraw-Hill.

Fletcher, D., & Sarkar, M. (2012). A grounded theory of psychological resilience in Olympic champions. *Psychology of Sport and Exercise, 13*(5), 669–678. https://doi.org/10.1016/j.psychsport.2012.04.007

Henriksen, K., Schinke, R. J., Moesch, K., McCann, S., Parham, W. D., Larsen, C. H., & Terry, P. (2020). Athlete mental health in the Olympic/Paralympic quadrennium: A multi-societal consensus statement. *International Journal of Sport and Exercise Psychology, 18*(3), 391–408. https://doi.org/10.1080/1612197X.2020.1746379

**Chapter 15: Sustainable high-performance cultures in sport**

Liverpool FC. How Jürgen Klopp creates a winning culture at LFC | Presented by Western Union [Internet]. YouTube. 2020. Available from: https://www.youtube.com/watch?v=sxrl0FP8vno

Papailiou A, Coates JK, Plateau CR, Gilmore H, Barker JB. A qualitative analysis of a positive elite Parasport performance culture. Adapted Physical Activity Quarterly [Internet]. 2023 May 9;41(1):9–32. Available from: https://doi.org/10.1123/apaq.2022-0108

Dawnay BO. Lionel Messi: Barcelona sold Deco and Ronaldinho in order to protect star player, claims ex-Arsenal man... talkSPORT [Internet]. 2019 Jun 27; Available from: https://talksport.com/football/565031/barcelona-deco-ronaldinho-drunk- alexander-hleb/

Cole J, Martin AJ. Developing a winning sport team culture: organisational culture in theory and practice. Sport in Society [Internet]. 2018 Feb 26;21(8):1204–22. Available from: https://doi.org/10.1080/17430437.2018.1442197

Fletcher D, Streeter A. A case study analysis of a high performance environment in elite swimming. Journal of Change Management [Internet]. 2016 Jan 14;16(2):123–41. Available from: https://doi.org/10.1080/14697017.2015.1128470

The organisational psychology of sport [Internet]. Routledge eBooks. 2016. Available from: https://doi.org/10.4324/9781315666532

Wagstaff C, Burton-Wylie S. Organisational Culture in Sport: A conceptual, Definitional, and Methodological review. Sport and Exercise Psychology Review [Internet]. 2018;14(2):32–52. Available from: https://researchportal.port.ac.uk/en/publications/organisational-culture-i n-sport-a-conceptual-definitional-and-met

Jones G, Gittins M, Hardy L. Creating an environment where high performance is inevitable and sustainable: the High Performance Environment model. Annual Review of High Performance Coaching & Consulting. 2009;139–49.

Turner AN, Bishop C, Cree J, Carr P, McCann A, Bartholomew B, et al. Building a High-Performance Model for Sport: A Human Development-Centered Approach. Strength and Conditioning Journal [Internet]. 2018 Dec 7;41(2):100–7. Available from: https://doi.org/10.1519/ssc.0000000000000447

Schein, E. Organisational culture and leadership. 1st ed. Jossey-Bass Publishers; 1992.

Humphrey J, Hughes D. High performance: Lessons from the Best on Becoming Your Best. Random House; 2021.

Baron J, Hannan M. Organisational blueprints for success in high-tech start-ups: Lessons from the Stanford Project on Emerging Companies. California Management Review. 2002;44(3):8–36.

Gamage M. Arsenal's club values remain their most admirable aspect. The Top Flight [Internet]. 2020 Apr 17; Available from: https://thetopflight.com/2020/04/17/arsenals-club-values-remain-admira ble-aspect/

Edmondson AC, Lei Z. Psychological Safety: the history, renaissance, and future of an interpersonal construct. Annual Review of Organisational Psychology and Organisational Behavior [Internet]. 2014

Jan 14;1(1):23–43. Available from: https://doi.org/10.1146/annurev-orgpsych-031413-091305

International Olympic Commitee. Mental Health in Elite Athletes Toolkit. International Olympic Commitee. 2021.

Smittick AL, Miner KN, Cunningham GB. The "I" in team: Coach incivility, coach gender, and team performance in women's basketball teams. Sport Management Review [Internet]. 2018 Jun 22;22(3):419–33. Available from: https://doi.org/10.1016/j.smr.2018.06.002

Morgan PBC, Fletcher D, Sarkar M. Developing team resilience: A season-long study of psychosocial enablers and strategies in a high-level sports team. Psychology of Sport and Exercise [Internet]. 2019 May 25;45:101543. Available from: https://doi.org/10.1016/j.psychsport.2019.101543

Fransen K, McEwan D, Sarkar M. The impact of identity leadership on team functioning and well-being in team sport: Is psychological safety the missing link? Psychology of Sport and Exercise [Internet]. 2020 Jul 22;51:101763. Available from: https://doi.org/10.1016/j.psychsport.2020.101763

Greenleaf RK. The servant as leader. Greanleef Publishing Center; 1970.

Burns. Leadership. Harper & Row; 1978.

Sky Sports Premier League. Jurgen Klopp's first Liverpool press conference: "I am the normal one" [Internet]. YouTube. 2015. Available from: https://www.youtube.com/watch?v=J-Re0BihMy4

Hogg MA. A social Identity Theory of leadership. Personality and Social Psychology Review [Internet]. 2001 Aug 1;5(3):184–200. Available from: https://doi.org/10.1207/s15327957pspr0503_1

Elberse A. Ferguson's Formula [Internet]. Harvard Business Review. 2018. Available from: https://hbr.org/2013/10/fergusons-formula

Haslam SA, Reicher SD, Platow MJ. The new psychology of leadership [Internet]. Routledge eBooks. 2020. Available from: https://doi.org/10.4324/9781351108232

OffTheBall. WATCH: Cristiano Ronaldo implores Portugal team-mate to take penalty in shootout. OffTheBall [Internet]. 2016 Jul 4; Available from:

https://www.offtheball.com/soccer/watch-cristiano-ronaldo-implores-portugal-teammate-to-take-penalty-in-shootout-268979

Scroll.in. When an injured Cristiano Ronaldo rallied Portugal to victory in Euro 2016 final from the sidelines. Scroll.in [Internet]. 2020 Jul 10; Available from:

https://scroll.in/field/967117/when-an-injured-cristiano-ronaldo-rallied-portugal-to-victory-in-euro-2016-final-from-the-sidelines

ESPNcricinfo. Tendulkar loss hard to cope with - Rohit. ESPNcricinfo [Internet]. 2013 Nov 16; Available from: https://www.espncricinfo.com/story/tendulkar-loss-hard-to-cope-with-roh it-689281

Future Generali - General Insurance. Mind Matters | EP. 1 – Sunil Chhetri [Internet]. YouTube. 2021. Available from: https://www.youtube.com/watch?v=d72NrBeDa48

**Note: Dr. Chris Harwood**

Harwood, C. (2008). Developmental consulting in a professional football academy: The 5Cs coaching efficacy program. *The Sport Psychologist*, *22*, 109-133

Harwood, C.G. & Anderson, R. (2015). *Coaching psychological skills in youth football: Developing the 5Cs.* Bennion-Kearney Publishers.

Hauser, L., Harwood, C.G., Honer, O., O'Connor, D. & Wachsmuth, S. (2022). Talent Development Environments within Sports: A Scoping Review examining Functional and Dysfunctional Environmental Features. *International Review of Sport and Exercise Psychology.* Advanced online publication

Martindale, R. J., Collins, D., & Daubney, J. (2005). Talent development: A guide for practice and research within sport. Quest, 57(4), 353-375